Paradise Restored

Paradise Restored

An Introduction to Bible Prophecy

Mark Sweetnam

WIPF & STOCK · Eugene, Oregon

Wipf and Stock Publishers
199 W 8th Ave, Suite 3
Eugene, OR 97401

Paradise Restored
An Introduction to Biblical Prophecy
By Sweetnam, Mark
Copyright © 2014 by Sweetnam, Mark All rights reserved.
Softcover ISBN-13: 978-1-7252-8928-4
Hardcover ISBN-13: 978-1-7252-8931-4
Publication date 10/16/2020
Previously published by Scripture Teaching Library (STL), 2014

This edition is a scanned facsimile of the original edition published in 2014.

※

Ye therefore, beloved, knowing these things before, take care
lest, being led away along with the error of the wicked,
ye should fall from your own stedfastness:
but grow in grace, and in the knowledge of
our Lord and Saviour Jesus Christ.
To Him be glory both now and
to the day of eternity.
Amen.

2 Peter 3:17–18, JND

※

Preface

THIS BOOK HAS ITS ORIGIN in the firm conviction that a grasp of God's prophetic programme is not an esoteric indulgence for the eccentric, but an essential element of every believer's knowledge of his or her Bible and an indispensable part of living a scriptural Christian life.

I am very thankful to God that this conviction was formed in my heart as a young believer, and very grateful for overseers in the assemblies in Skibbereen and Rathmines for their exercise and care to ensure that prophetic truth was clearly and regularly taught, and for faithful servants of God who generously imparted the fruits of their careful study of God's Word. Reading through the pages, I am struck afresh by the scale of the debt I owe to these teachers, and I am glad to have the opportunity to acknowledge this debt in print.

I am grateful, too, to the elders in Rathmines for the opportunity to teach through much of this material in the Sunday School, and to the boys and girls – and older ones – for their enthusiastic and encouraging response to the subject.

Much of the material contained in these pages first appeared in print in *Truth & Tidings*, and another time I would like to record my indebtedness to Sandy Higgins for his generous invitation to contribute, for his continuing editorial patience, and for his permission to reprint the articles in this form. Chapters 5, 21, and 22 were first published in *Assembly Testimony*, and I would like to thank Brian Currie for his permission to reuse this material.

Finally, I would like to thank the brethren who share in the work of the Scripture Teaching Library for all their encouragement and fellowship, and for their helpful comments on the manuscript of this volume.

It is my prayer that God will use this book to His glory, and that it might stimulate its readers to a greater interest in the study of prophecy.

MARK SWEETNAM
Dublin, 2014

CONTENTS

1	Why Prophecy Matters	13
2	When Prophecy Becomes History	19
3	The Backbone of Prophecy	27
4	The Rapture	33
5	'We Shall Be Like Him'	41
6	The Judgement Seat of Christ	45
7	The Marriage of the Lamb	51
8	In the Throne Room of Eternity	57
9	The Commencement of the Tribulation	63
10	The Character of the Tribulation	69
11	The Course of the Tribulation	75
12	Towards Armageddon	81
13	The Return of the King	87
14	The Glorious Appearing	93
15	The Certainty of the Millennium	99
16	The Character of the Millennium	105
17	The Citizens and Conditions of the Millennium	111

18	The Conclusion of the Millennium	117
19	The Great White Throne	123
20	The Eternal State	128
21	The Hope that is in You	133
22	'Able to Give an Answer'	139
23	Conclusion	145
	Appendix: The Days of Scripture	151

Except where otherwise indicated, all quotations from Scripture are taken from Thomas Newberry's edition of the Authorised (King James) Version.

Chapter One

Why Prophecy Matters

Predicting the future is a human obsession. Businesses invest heavily in the services of analysts who identify the hottest trends. Scientists design complex mathematical models that can be used to formulate predictions about the world, and the universe. Philosophers and sociologists ponder the future of humanity. And countless men and women consult fortune-tellers, psychics and astrologers in the vain hope that the prognostications that they offer may be of some value in directing their lives and guiding their decisions. The future, it has justly been said, is big business.

But though we are greatly concerned by the future, we understand very little about it. The failure of politicians, pundits, or prophetic pretenders to anticipate global financial turmoil is only the most recent evidence of our inability to predict the course that events will take, or the nature and magnitude of the forces that direct them. Time and again, confidently proclaimed predictions have to be retracted, red faces hidden, and generous helpings of humble pie downed. Experts and amateurs, scientists and charlatans alike have to acknowledge that they are wrong far more often than they are right.

These failures are inevitable because we are temporal beings, immersed in time, and finite beings limited in our knowledge. As such, we lack the ability to stand outside the flow of events and to obtain a stable perspective from which to make sense of time. Our intellects can only embrace a tiny fraction of the complex forces and factors that shape events. A definitive account of the future can only be provided by someone who stands outside of time, and who can see every cause, from the vagaries of individual whim to the violence of global conflict or catastrophe.

It is astounding to think that we do have an account of the future provided by One Who is outside of time, and Who has a comprehensive insight into every action and reaction. It is still more astounding to remember that this account comes not just from a spectator – however privileged – but from the great Creator and Orchestrator, the 'King of the ages' (1 Tim. 1:17, *JND*) Who not only 'made the world and all things therein' (Acts 17:24), but Who 'made the ages' (Heb. 1:2 *Weymouth*). And it is not only astounding, but confounding too, that humanity in general, and even so many Christians, have so little time for that revelation, and make so little effort to comprehend and understand the Divine preview of human history.

The study of Biblical prophecy has often been seen as an eccentric occupation, best left to those on – or approaching – the lunatic fringe. Such a perception is difficult to excuse or explain, and is very harmful for any believer who hopes to achieve a balanced and comprehensive understanding of God's Word.

It is important to recognize that prophecy is pervasive. If I decide that I am not interested in the study of prophecy, I deprive myself of a proper understanding of large portions of Scripture, both the Old Testament and the New. And in doing so, I implicitly call into question the wisdom of God, Who included such an amount, and such a diversity, of prophecy in His revealed Word. If our Bibles are to make sense to us, we need to make sense of prophecy.

We need also to appreciate that prophecy is precious. In it God takes us into His confidence, and graciously outlines His blueprint for the future. This, as the Lord Jesus pointed out to His disciples, is the act of a friend (Jn 15:15) and to treat this revelation as something inessential or bothersome is to betray an unbecoming failure to appreciate the honour that God has conferred upon us.

In addition, God's Word demonstrates clearly that prophecy is preservative and protective. A grasp of Biblical prophecy is a prophylactic against a number of serious ills. Scripture itself demonstrates that this is so – the New Testament provides us with important examples of the impact that confusion about prophecy can have on the life of the believer.

Two believers walked the road to Emmaus on the third day after the crucifixion of the Lord Jesus. As Jesus Himself drew near, and went with them, He commented on their most striking feature – they were sad. The cause of this sadness? Their friend and leader had been crucified, but even more devastating than this was the overthrow of all their expectations. In despair they lamented 'we trusted that it had been He which should have redeemed Israel' (Lk. 24:21). A failure to understand prophecy had robbed these believers of their joy. And in their need, the risen Lord ministered not to their emotions but to their minds, and that most robustly. Describing them as 'fools, and slow of heart to believe all that the prophets have spoken' (v. 25), He embarked on an exposition of Scriptural prophecy that must have thrilled these despairing believers to their very core. Small wonder that their hearts burned as the Saviour Himself brought their defective understanding of prophecy into line with the teaching of Scripture.

Some decades later, the apostle Paul wrote to the assembly in Thessalonica. He anticipated that their grasp of prophetic truth would soon come under attack from false teachers. Paul is very clear about the potential effects of this error, and beseeches the believers that they would not be 'shaken in mind, or be troubled' (2 Thess. 2:2). To go astray on prophecy would rob them of their peace. In the face of this threat, Paul fortifies the minds of the believers with an exposition of prophetic truth. And it was not only the Thessalonians whose peace was ensured by a firm grasp of the prophetic programme. The word translated 'troubled' occurs in only two other places in Scripture (Mt. 24:6; Mk 13:7) and in both of these passages we find the Lord Jesus unfolding prophetic truth that will preserve the peace of His own.

The Thessalonians were not the only assembly in Scripture to be affected by prophetic myopia. Just a few years later, Paul had to write to the Corinthians. Problems abounded at Corinth, but the apostle chose to deal first with the problem of divisions in the assembly. While serious in themselves, those divisions were only the symptom of deeper difficulties and, like a skilled diagnostician, Paul traces their root in the carnality and worldliness of the Corinthians. And, in chapter 4 of the epistle, he highlights the Corinthians' confusion about their place in prophecy as one of the sources of their diminished spiritual stature. The Corinthians had 'reigned as kings' (1 Cor. 4:8), demonstrating a failure to understand their place within the prophetic programme. And that failure had robbed them of their separation.

Like so many whose views about the Millennium are unscriptural, they had come to view the world as a neutral space, where Christians, making use of worldly wisdom, and worldly means of persuasion, could compete on an equal footing with contemporary philosophers. But Paul reminds them that they have mistaken the character of the age. Using imagery from Roman circuses, he makes it clear that there is no neutral ground – the Corinthians were either seated as spectators, or fighting for their lives in the sands of the arena. The time for reigning has not yet come, and Paul pleads for these believers to grasp the proper progression of prophecy, and become his followers, even if they followed him to shame and to death.

These passages confirm for us that prophecy is intensely practical. Understanding the detail of God's plan for the future is no abstruse intellectual exercise. Rather, it has – or should have – enormous impact upon how we live our lives. Large companies pay dearly for the services of analysts and experts because they understand that their insights about the future will help to inform their priorities and investments in the present. In a similar, though far greater way, prophecy allows us to live the present in the light of the future, to understand God's plan for the planet and for us, and thus to decide our priorities and values in the light of what is really and enduringly important.

Chapter Two

When Prophecy Becomes History

Prophecy pervades Scripture. From the protoevangelical promise of the Seed of the woman Who would bruise the serpent's head (Gen. 3:15), to the final 'Surely I come quickly' (Rev. 22:20), God's Word has a great deal to say about the future. The prophecies of Scripture touch on many great events, but these first and final prophecies summarize the two momentous events that are the focal points of God's plan for creation and the chief preoccupation of prophecy. 'The testimony of Jesus is the spirit of prophecy' (Rev. 19:10). It is the essence of prophecy to present Christ and the first and second comings of the Lord Jesus Christ are the preeminent subjects of prophetic revelation.

In the dispensation of grace, we are in a unique position in relation to these great events. We, 'on whom the ends of the ages have come' (1 Cor. 10:11, *NET*) are living in the period between these comings. As such, much that was prophecy for previous ages is history for us. Thus, we are in an unparalleled position to understand how prophecy works, to learn from the fulfilment of prophecies of the first coming principles that illuminate and invigorate our understanding of the way in which God causes His prophetic word to come to pass.

The record of Scripture leaves absolutely no room for any doubt that the fulfilment of prophecy is certain. What God says will happen will inevitably come to pass. And this is true, no matter what the opposition to His purpose or the apparent impossibility of His promises. From the moment that God articulated the promise of the coming conquering woman's Seed, all of Satan's energy and ingenuity were marshalled to thwart the fulfilment of the prophecy. But no matter what his efforts, God's great prophetic programme moved serenely and inexorably forward until 'when the fulness of the time was come' (Gal. 4:4), the Son of God became the Seed of the woman and, at the cross, bruised the serpent's head. Even apart from the machinations of the enemy, the accomplishment of prophecy required tremendous difficulties to be overcome. Again and again, God has seen to it that His fulfilment of prophecy demonstrates His omnipotent power. So Abraham must wait until the birth of a son was naturally impossible before God's promise is performed and a son is born to one 'as good as dead' (Heb. 11:12). Following Pharaoh's defiance, God will harden his heart until only a remarkable sequence of miraculous events can pry His people free. God will place His finger upon the mighty Caesar to ensure that Christ would be born in Bethlehem of Judaea. And when the time came for the Messiah to be born, natural probability and possibility are alike set aside for 'Behold, a virgin shall conceive, and bear a Son' (Isa. 7:14).

The fulfilment of God's prophetic word is not a matter of probability or of chance. The certainty of prophecy is underwritten by the immensity of His power. Abraham had a far less comprehensive revelation of God than we do, but what he did know was a sufficient basis for him to be 'fully persuaded that, what [God] had promised, He was able also to perform' (Rom. 4:21). We have seen prophecy that has become history, witnessed the way in which God's promises have been performed. As we consider prophecy that is as yet unfulfilled, we ought also to be fully persuaded of the certainty of God's Word, knowing that what He has promised He will inevitably perform.

The fulfilment of prophecy, then, is certain. But it is also comprehensive. The first prophecy, in Genesis 3, provided a very broad-brush outline of God's purpose. In the centuries that followed that picture would be filled in with a mass of intricate detail. The prophets of the Old Testament made a wealth of predictions, covering everything from the place and manner of the Saviour's birth to the timing and mode of His death and the reality of His resurrection. And each and every prophecy was fulfilled. Even as He hung on the cross, the Saviour's priority was the fulfilment of prophecy. Even as He knew that the work of atonement had been accomplished, He was concerned to ensure that no detail of prophecy would be disregarded or left unfulfilled: 'After this, Jesus knowing that all things were now accomplished, that the scripture might be fulfilled, saith, I thirst' (Jn 19:28).

In this regard, too, the first advent of Christ has provided the template for the way in which prophecy is to be fulfilled. God has not provided us with the sort of vague and generalised outline in which modern predictors and prognosticators take refuge. Rather, He has given us just as detailed and definite an account of the events that will precede and attend the second coming of Christ as He did of those that accompanied His first advent. And, just as the earlier prophecies, in all their complex detail, were fulfilled, so too will those that still await their accomplishment.

The record of history also confirms that prophecy is fulfilled clearly. Interpreters of Biblical prophecy, from a range of ecclesiastical persuasions, have often been guilty of treating Scripture like a code that needs to be cracked. Prophecies about the future are allegorised and spiritualised until they lose any literal meaning and much or all of their practical import. But this was not the way in which prophecy worked at the first coming of the Saviour. Think of the wise men. They came to Jerusalem, having seen the star in the East, and asked in Herod's palace 'Where is He that is born King of the Jews?' (Mt. 2:2). When a troubled Herod gathered together the chief priests and scribes, and put the question to them, they had no doubt about where to look. Their immediate recourse was to prophetic Scripture:

> And they said unto him, In Bethlehem of Judaea: for thus it is written by the prophet, And thou Bethlehem, in the land of Juda, art not the least among the princes of Juda: for out of thee shall come a Governor, that shall rule My people Israel (Mt. 2:5–6).

And, having identified the relevant passage, they did not subject it to any fanciful spiritual interpretation. Their answer to the question assumed that Scripture meant what it said, that Bethlehem meant Bethlehem, and Juda meant Juda.

Another example of the importance of literally interpreting prophecy is found in Psalm 22:18. The entirety of this Psalm is a wonderful prediction of the scenes of the Saviour's death. Verse 16, in particular, is remarkable for the clarity with which it described the gruesome process of crucifixion: 'they pierced My hands and My feet.' The words are remarkable for more than their clarity. This Psalm was written by King David, whose reign is generally dated to about 1040–970 BC. Yet crucifixion is only recorded from the sixth century BC. The implications of this are striking and unavoidable. Four hundred years before the Persians devised this peculiarly agonizing method of execution, David had prophesied its most distinctive features. One hardly likes to imagine what some contemporary interpreters of prophecy would have done with the passage had they not had the benefit of hindsight. But, though no one at the time could have understood exactly how the verse would come to pass, God's Word was fulfilled with the utmost precision.

Examples could be multiplied to prove the point. God speaks to us literally in His Word, and He means us to take Him at His word. This does not mean that we disregard metaphors, or fail to take account of poetic language or of symbolism. It does, however, mean that we have no licence to allegorize or spiritualize prophecy – or any other part of Scripture – either because we do not understand it, or because we do not wish to yield to its teaching. Rather, we are bound to accept the literal truth of what Scripture says and to apply to prophetic Scripture the normal rules of interpretation that we apply to any other text.

The witness of Scripture is irrefutable – prophecy is to be interpreted literally. And this is no minor or pedantic point. Our willingness or our failure to allow this fundamental principle to guide our interpretation of Scripture has profound implications for our understanding of Scripture. If the Bible means what it says, it follows that when Scripture says Israel, it means Israel. There is no passage that gives us even the smallest of hints that Israel is ever synonymous with the Church, or that it means anything other than the literal, earthly nation, and the men and women who trace their descent from Abraham, Isaac, and Jacob.

Once we grasp this fact, we begin to appreciate that most prophecy does not directly apply to the Church at all. Indeed, given that the truth of the Church is a mystery, which lay unrevealed in the heart of God until New Testament times (Eph. 3:3–7), it is clear that none of Old Testament prophecy, in all its diversity and detail, speaks of the Church.

It also becomes clear that God's plans for Israel are very different to those that He has for the Church. Old Testament prophecy speaks of physical and terrestrial blessing, of the reign on earth of the Lord Jesus Christ. The blessings promised to the Church are of a different order. They are heavenly, rather than earthly, and spiritual, rather than physical. And, if we are interpreting Scripture literally, that distinction must be maintained – we cannot allegorise the earthly promises of the Old Testament in an effort to make them seem more suitably spiritual for the Church.

In the light of this, it becomes clear that God's prophetic purpose is not monolithic. He has a plan for the Church. He also has a plan for Israel. Those plans are distinct and distinctive, and we must not confuse them, or our grasp of prophecy will be fatally compromised.

An insistence upon the literal interpretation of Scripture, and a consequent recognition of the difference between Israel and the Church, and the distinctiveness of their role in God's purpose are fundamental to the interpretation of prophecy provided in this book.[*] The outline that is presented in the

---

[*] These are also the essential elements of dispensationalism. It is not the purpose of this book to provide a full explanation or defence of

following chapters emerges from the application of these principles.

2 Peter 1:19 speaks of 'a more sure word of prophecy'. In this remarkable passage, Peter elevates the certainty of prophetic Scripture above that which he saw and heard of the ministry of the Lord, and even above the utterances of the heavenly voice. There could be no more emphatic endorsement of the accuracy, reliability, and perspicuity of the Word of God. As we think of the way in which prophecy has become history may we rejoice again in the wisdom, the might, and the greatness of God, being fully persuaded that what He has promised, He is able, also, to perform.

---

dispensationalism. For a fuller account see Mark Sweetnam, *The Dispensations: God's Plan for the Ages*, (Cookstown: Scripture Teaching Library, 2013).

Chapter Three

The Backbone of Prophecy

The student of prophecy finds himself in a similar position to someone who is completing a jigsaw puzzle. While the pieces of prophetic revelation are not scattered randomly or haphazardly, they are found throughout Scripture. Each is vital in its own right, but each needs to be correctly placed in relation to all the others so that we obtain a clear picture of God's great prophetic programme. Even the most casual of jigsaw builders will know how useful it is to have the picture on the box to hand, and how much more difficult the puzzle becomes without that orientating overview. The Bible student, too, will find his task made immeasurably easier if he has in mind a framework that explains how all the different pieces fit together into one Divine masterpiece. We find just such an overview in Daniel 9.

Daniel 9 has been described as 'the backbone of prophecy'. Understanding this chapter is a vital part of getting prophecy right. If we misinterpret these verses, we will quickly find ourselves attempting to complete one jigsaw with the pieces from another and, in our frustration, resorting to cutting bits off the pieces, and otherwise forcing them to fit in. But this chapter is not just valuable for the great prophetic outline that it contains. In it, Daniel demonstrates how we ought to approach the study of prophetic Scripture, and it is worthwhile briefly to consider the context, as well as the content, of the revelation that he received.

Firstly we should notice Daniel's attitude. This is outlined in the words of the angel in the following chapter. Michael speaks of how Daniel 'set [his] heart to understand' (10:12). Daniel was not prepared to tolerate gaps in his knowledge of God's purpose. Rather, he had a committed heart and an engaged mind. And his attitude did not go unrewarded. The archangel came to make him understand (v. 14). God rewards those who set their heart to understand His Word.

Daniel's attitude was expressed in the attention that he gave to Scripture. The opening verses of chapter 9 demonstrate that Daniel had grasped the vital truth that an understanding of God's will must be based upon the study of God's Word. This is an essential lesson for us all to learn. Faced with a difficult subject like prophecy, it is all too easy for us to resort to and rely on other books. They have their place – it is a foolish Christian who disdains the help provided by the writings of Godly men. But the focus of our study must always be Scripture, and it is to God's Word that we must pay close and careful attention.

To this attention to Scripture Daniel added an approach to God in prayer. Daniel's supplication is one of the great pattern prayers of Scripture, and deserves careful study in its own right. But we should notice his confession of sin, his confidence in God's character and in His Word, and his call for God to deliver His people. Would that our study of Scripture would move us to a similar response.

Daniel's prayer received a most remarkable answer in the appearance of the angel and the announcement of a concise but crucial outline of prophecy. Gabriel unfolded a programme of 'seventy weeks'.

THE DESIGNATION OF THE WEEKS

Most English translations have Gabriel speaking of seventy weeks. However, the underlying Hebrew word simply means a series of seven, and for this reason, some commentators speak of seventy heptads, or hebdomads. When the word is used we must look to the context to discover precisely what the series of seven in question is made up of.

THE DURATION OF THE WEEKS

To determine the duration of the seventy sevens foretold to Daniel, we rely on two important passages of Scripture. In Daniel 7:25 the events that follow the breaking of the covenant in the middle of the seventieth week are said to last for 'a time and times and the dividing of a time', or a year + two years + half a year. In Revelation 12:14, the same period is described as lasting for 1,260 days (a Biblical year has 360 days, and 360 × 3.5 = 1,260). Comparing Daniel 9 with other passages of Scripture demonstrates clearly that Gabriel is speaking of seventy sevens of years, or four hundred and ninety years.*

THE DIVISION OF THE WEEKS

Gabriel's announcement divides the seventy weeks or four hundred and ninety years into three portions, consisting, respectively, of seven, sixty-two, and one seven-year periods. The first two periods cover the period 'from the going forth of the commandment to

---

* Within the scope of this chapter, only a sketchy overview of this great subject has been possible. Readers who wish to look in greater depth at the calculations involved will find further recommended reading in the final chapter of this book.

restore and to build Jerusalem' (v. 25) until the cutting off of Messiah. Historically, this covers the period from March 5, 444 BC (Neh. 2:1), to March 30, AD 33, the date of Christ's triumphal entry into Jerusalem. With meticulous precision and miraculous accuracy, the Saviour moved to keep the appointment of prophecy, fulfilling to the day the programme outlined to Daniel. Following the death of Christ, 'the people of the prince that shall come' (Dan. 9:26) did indeed destroy the city. The forces of the Roman general Titus stormed the walls of Jerusalem in AD 70, devastating the city and razing the sanctuary, just as prophecy foretold.

This detail alerts the careful reader to one of the most important features of these weeks, namely the fact that the seventieth week does not follow directly from the end of the sixty-ninth. Notice that the Temple – the sanctuary – is destroyed after the end of the sixty-ninth week (v. 26). This happened in AD 70, and brought the offering of Jewish sacrifice to an abrupt, and so far total, end. Yet, we read that, in the middle of the seventieth week, 'the prince that shall come' will 'cause the sacrifice and the oblation to cease' (vv. 26–27). Evidently, then, there must be a gap in the seventy weeks in which, amongst other things, the Temple is rebuilt and sacrifice resumed.

Commentators sometimes speak of this gap as the prophetic parenthesis. This reflects the fact that the period from the death of Christ to the beginning of the Tribulation – the Church age or the dispensation of grace – is not revealed anywhere in prophetic Scripture. Because in grammatical terms a parenthesis is not essential to the meaning of a sentence some commentators have suggested that this terminology represents an under-valuing of the importance of the Church age. To draw such a conclusion is unwarranted, but we avoid running the risk of such confusion by using scriptural language, and referring to the Church age as a mystery – long concealed, but now revealed – rather than as a parenthesis.*

The final heptad of years is divided into two three-and-a-half year periods. The first half is the Tribulation, when Divine judgement is poured out upon an apostate and Christ-rejecting earth. This period is marked by the emergence of Antichrist – 'the prince that shall come' – and by the resumption of Jewish worship under his protection. The second period, the Great Tribulation, or 'the time of Jacob's trouble' (Jer. 30:7), will begin when Antichrist breaks his protective treaty, and Israel becomes once more the object of intense persecution by the nations of the earth. This persecution will culminate in the siege of Jerusalem, and the triumphant return to earth of the glorified Lord Jesus, Who will destroy the rebels and establish His righteous kingdom for a thousand years.

THE DOMAIN OF THE WEEKS

Both Daniel's prayer and its answer focus on Israel and Jerusalem. Daniel prays to God for 'the city which is called by Thy name' (v. 18), and Gabriel informs him that 'seventy weeks are determined upon thy people and upon thy holy city' (v. 24). This prophetic framework, then, does not refer to the Church or to individual believers of this age. We have our own unique – and uniquely important – place in God's plan, but we do not have a part in the prophetic programme outlined in these verses.

---

* See, for example, Rom. 16:25 and Eph. 3:3–4.

THE DETERMINATION OF THE WEEKS

The prophetic programme summarised in this chapter has been carefully designed by God, with definite aims in view: 'Seventy weeks are determined ... to finish the transgression, and to make an end of sins, and to make reconciliation for iniquity, and to bring in everlasting righteousness, and to seal up the vision and prophecy, and to anoint the most holy' (v. 24). God is never caught out by circumstances. His perfect plan was determined far in advance. The first sixty-nine weeks of years have come to pass with perfect precision, just as He determined. The remaining week, too, will unfold, just as He has said. And, just as the events will take place punctually, His great purpose for His people will be inexorably worked out. An end will be brought to sin and idolatry, prophecy will be fulfilled, and the King Who was 'cut off and had nothing' (v. 26, marg.) will be anointed and enthroned as the 'Most Holy'. 'His rich designs most carefully are woven, There are with Him no loose or broken ends.'*

---

* Winifred A. Iverson, 'The Lord will perfect that which doth concern me', *The Believers Hymn Book*, 453.

Chapter Four

The Rapture

On the eve of His crucifixion, the Lord Jesus and His apostles gathered in the upper room. The night was dark, and sinister forces were in operation. In just a few hours, the Saviour would be arrested, tried, and condemned, led out to the place of execution, and would suffer an agonising death that spoke of rejection and shame. The men who gathered with the Lord were about to experience the most traumatic and trying hours and days of their lives. And knowing all this, He spoke to reassure them: 'Let not your heart be troubled' (Jn 14:1).

On the lips of any other man these words would have been the worst of platitudes. But it was the Lord Who spoke, and, in the moments that followed, He outlined the resources that gave meaning to His reassurance. He would speak of a place prepared, of His person, of His prayer, of the Paraclete, of His presence, and His peace. Much of what He unfolded introduced new aspects of familiar truth, but the promise He made to His disciples was distinctively new. 'If I go and prepare a place for you', He declared, 'I will come again and receive you unto Myself, that where I am, there ye may be also' (Jn 14:3).

With these words of promise, the Saviour introduced the great hope of His imminent and personal return for

His own. The disciples would have known that Christ would one day be manifest in power and glory to subdue His enemies and establish His kingdom, but this return was something different, unique in its immediacy, and unique in its purpose.

This event has come to be known as the 'Rapture'. Though this term is not found in Scripture, it effectively conveys the nature of the event. We use it now most often to describe a transport of delight, but the Latin word at its root means 'to snatch away', and was originally used to describe the actions of an invading army that would swoop down, and grab people and property. It provides a vivid picture of the suddenness and swiftness of the Lord's return to remove His people from the enemy's territory.

It is this suddenness that is emphasised in the Lord's promise. The return that He describes is an imminent one – it could happen at any moment. He mentions only one condition to be fulfilled before the Rapture can take place – His going away. From the moment that He returned to heaven, every precondition for His return had been accomplished. And the imminence of His return is confirmed by the grammar of the passage. The verb phrase translated 'I will come again' is in the present tense, and could be translated as 'I am coming again'. The Lord Jesus did not encourage His own with the promise of His return at some remote point in the future. Rather, He ensured that even the darkest and most difficult days that they passed through would be enlightened by the thought that at any moment He would return, with the tender purpose to receive them to Himself. And that hope remains for us today. The return of our Lord could take place at any moment, and this radiant hope should cast its transforming glow over every aspect and facet of our lives.

The truth of the Rapture, revealed by the Lord in John 14, is developed in Paul's epistles. Writing to the Thessalonians, he deals with the programme of the Rapture. The Thessalonians were concerned that believers who had already died had missed the Rapture. Paul writes to ensure that that they would not sorrow, as those who had no hope. And, as he outlines the Rapture programme, which he himself received 'by the word of the Lord' (1 Thess. 4:15), he stresses that 'the living, who remain to the coming of the Lord, are in no way to anticipate those who have fallen asleep' (v. 15, JND). He demonstrates this by giving us the most detailed account of the Rapture that we find in our Bibles.

The events that Paul describes are dramatic – the archangelic shout and the trumpet of the Lord. This great clamour will go unheard and unheeded by the majority on earth. But its call will reach the ears of those who are 'in Christ'. First the dead and then the living will rise 'to meet the Lord in the air' (v. 17).

In the spiritual realm, too, the impact of this tumult will be tremendous. The Saviour will triumphantly invade the sphere of Satan's influence and, as 'the prince of the power of the air' (Eph. 2:2) stands impotently by, Christ will marshal the serried ranks of those whom He has loved and Satan has hated. And those who gather will not only reflect the glory of Christ, but will be transformed to share it. There, in the air, grace will reach a grand climax, and Satan will taste anew the bitterness of his irretrievable rout at Calvary.

Notwithstanding the drama of the scene, the detail that should most thrill the hearts of the redeemed is its intimacy. It is 'the Lord Himself' (1 Thess. 4:16) Who comes to claim His own. When the time comes to re-gather scattered Israel He will 'send His angels, and ... gather together His elect' (Mk 13:27), but for the rapturing of His

Church, for the calling of His bride, no emissary will suffice. 'The Lord Himself' is coming for us.

The Thessalonians had been confused about the programme of the Rapture, but the truth of Christ's return for His own was not new to them. Indeed, 1 Thessalonians 1:10 confirms the central importance that the Rapture had for these believers. They had 'turned to God, from idols' and become workers and watchers. They began 'to serve the living and true God' and 'to wait for His Son from heaven, Whom He raised from the dead' (vv. 9–10). And Paul expands on this, not because the Thessalonians had any doubt the identity of God's Son, but in order to stress the preservation associated with the Rapture. The coming Son of God is 'Jesus, our deliverer from the coming wrath' (v. 10, JND). Paul is not saying that because the Thessalonians had trusted Christ they would never be in hell – wonderful though that truth was. Rather, he is reminding them that Jesus is their Saviour from the Tribulation, the seven-year period when God's wrath will be poured out on the earth in a cataclysm of suffering. In those awful days the Church has no place, 'for God hath not appointed us to wrath, but to obtain salvation by our Lord Jesus Christ' (1 Thess. 5:9). Like Enoch, we will be snatched away before judgement breaks, preserved from the wrath to come.

When Paul speaks of the Rapture to the Corinthians, it is the power of the event that he stresses. Addressing their error, he demonstrates the link that exists between Christ's resurrection and that of believers. To doubt one is to deny the other – Christ's resurrection is the prototype and proof of ours. But the power of the resurrection has implications for the living as well as for the dead. The apostle is unfolding a mystery, concealed in earlier ages. And that mystery is the truth of the Rapture: 'We shall not all sleep, but we shall all be changed. In a moment, in the twinkling of an eye, at the last trump' (1 Cor. 15:51–52). What a mighty impact God's resurrecting power will have in that instant – 'the dead shall be raised incorruptible, and we shall be changed'. 'In a flash, at a trumpet's crash' every defect, every trace of death's dark dominion will be obliterated, and we shall share our Saviour's glory.

The Rapture is a practical truth. The hope that our Lord is coming for us, and the consciousness that He could come at any moment should shape our priorities, our values, and our actions, and should stir us to live every day for Him, as though it were the last we had to give. And it is a precious truth, which should stir our hearts, charge our consciences, and cause us to ever live on tiptoes of expectation, knowing that our blessed Lord is coming quickly.

But, even as we rejoice in the preciousness of the Rapture and all that it will mean for us, let us not forget what this event will mean for Christ, and the unique worth that is has for Him.

CHRIST'S PRAYER ANSWERED

It is unwise to claim that any passage of Scripture has outstanding importance – all the Word of God is necessary, precious, and sacred. Nonetheless, we cannot help but feel, as we come to John 17, that we stand on exceptionally holy ground. In the very shadows of Calvary, we are privileged to hear the Lord Jesus pray, and are given a most precious insight into His desires for His own. He asks many wonderful things for His people; among them this tremendous request: 'Father, I will that they also, whom Thou hast given Me, be with Me where I am; that they may behold My glory, which Thou hast given Me: for Thou lovedst Me before the foundation of the world' (v. 24). This prayer is answered in part whenever a believer is called home, and is 'absent from the body', and 'present with the Lord' (2 Cor. 5:8). But, in its fullest sense, Christ's prayer, encompassing all the redeemed of this age, has yet to be answered. Two millennia have passed since the words were spoken. But delay is not denial, and the prayer of Christ for His own will be answered when all that have been given to Him 'shall see Him as He is' (1 Jn 3:2).

CHRIST'S PROMISE ACCOMPLISHED

A little earlier that Passover evening, dark clouds were already beginning to gather. The betrayer had gone forth, and Peter's denial had been prophesied. In this atmosphere of darkness and defeat – the very hour of the power of darkness – the Saviour gave His disciples a bright word of comfort, and a promise:

> Let not your heart be troubled: ye believe in God, believe also in Me. In My Father's house are many mansions: if it were not so, I would have told you. I go to prepare a place for you. And if I go and prepare a place for you, I will come again, and receive you unto Myself; that where I am, there ye may be also. (Jn 14:1–3).

In the circumstances, it was understandable that the disciples should focus more on His going, but for us, it is the fact of His coming – immediate, imminent, and eagerly awaited – that shines most brightly in these verses. He has promised, and the words of confidence that Naomi spoke about Boaz's promise are even more appropriate to our heavenly Boaz: He 'will not be in rest, until he have finished the thing this day' (Ruth 3:18).

CHRIST'S PURCHASE ACQUIRED

We who are saved are 'redeemed ... with the precious blood of Christ' (1 Pet. 1:18–19). The price of our redemption was fully paid at Calvary – Christ's work was not a down payment. But, while the price of our redemption has been fully paid, our redemption itself is not complete. Ephesians reminds us that we have been 'sealed with that holy Spirit of promise, which is the earnest of our inheritance until the redemption of the purchased possession' (Eph. 1:13–14) Indeed, it is this very truth that Paul turns to in Romans 8 to illustrate the fact that hope looks forward to the accomplishment of Divine promises. In that passage, we are seen as those 'which have the firstfruits of the Spirit, even we ourselves groan within ourselves, waiting for the adoption, to wit, the redemption of our body. For we are saved by hope' (vv. 23–24). The price has been completely paid. The purchase has been sealed, marked as Christ's. But the moment is still to come when He will claim His purchase, and finally acquire that which He prized so highly that He 'sold all that He had, and bought it' (Mt. 13:46)

For the believer, then, the Rapture is a present and a precious hope. It should be ever before us, filling our horizons, constantly occupying our expectation, determining our values, and affecting our lives. But we are not alone in our longing for it to take place. With a longing greater than we can understand or share, our Saviour too waits and wishes for the moment when His prayer will be answered, His promise accomplished, His purchase acquired, and His bride brought to Himself.

Chapter Five

'WE SHALL BE LIKE HIM'

I JOHN 3:2 CONTAINS A GLORIOUS PROMISE for the believer when it states that, at Christ's appearing, 'we shall see Him as He is.' This is a wonderful truth – not just that we will see Christ, but that we will see Him 'as He is', with no distorting filter, with no infirmity of sight. What a thrilling prospect this is: we will see the One 'Whom having not seen, [we] love' (1 Pet. 1:8). But what is truly remarkable about John's promise that we will see the Lord Jesus is that it is only part of the programme that he outlines in the opening verses of chapter 3. To see Him will be wonderful, but our hope does not stop there. Rather, the apostle looks above and beyond this, and scales the heights of God's purpose for His people, asserting categorically and unconditionally that 'we know that, when He shall appear, we shall be like Him' (v. 2). God wants us to see His Son, to be with His Son, but, best of all, He desires and ordains that we should be like His Son.

THE CERTAINTY OF THE CHANGE

For the believer, it sometimes seems an unthinkable thing that this could ever happen. We are conscious of the flawless perfection of Christ and of failing and weakness within. Physically and spiritually imperfect, we wonder that ever we should be able to be like Him. But like Him we shall be: this hope carries all the power and assurance of Divine purpose and promise. Romans 8:29 brings before us very forcibly the certainty of this change: 'whom He did foreknow, He also did predestinate to be conformed to the image of His Son, that He might be the firstborn among many brethren.' Likeness to Christ is not an optional extra; it is not the aspiration of God for some of His people. Rather, it is the destination, clear and certain, for which He has marked us out. Notice, too, that this certainty is linked with God's purpose for Christ – 'that He might be the firstborn among many brethren'.

A similar emphasis can be seen in Philippians 3:21:

> For our conversation is in heaven; from whence also we look for the Saviour, the Lord Jesus Christ: Who shall change our vile body, that it may be fashioned like unto His glorious body, according to the working whereby He is able even to subdue all things unto Himself.

Why, we might ask, is it not the power of resurrection that is stressed in these verses? Surely it is because we have already discovered, in chapter 2 of Philippians, that God has committed Himself to the glorification of His Son, so that 'every knee should bow... and every tongue should confess that Jesus Christ is Lord' (vv. 10–11). For the prospect of our change to the image of Christ to be underwritten by God's promise to us would be all the certainty we would require. God has gone further, however, and linked our future with that of His Son, and our transformation is doubly certain, because of God's promise to us, and because of His promise to Christ.

CHRONOLOGY OF THE CHANGE

All of the hopes of the believer have definite implications for the present – this, indeed, is one of the hallmarks of true hope. But the hope of likeness to Christ is unusual in its chronology. It is a comprehensive hope: Romans 8 connects it to our past, and Philippians and 1 John link it with our future. But as well as being a goal ordained in the past, and a glorious certainty of our future, it is a process on-going in the life of the believer presently. Consider 2 Corinthians 3:18: 'But we all, with open face beholding as in a glass the glory of the Lord, are changed into the same image from glory to glory, even as by the Spirit of the Lord.' This verse speaks of a change that is happening right now, in the life of every believer. That change is incremental, but it is also inevitable. In our experience it can be hard to recognise, and seem frustratingly gradual, and few of us would claim to have made the progress we ought to have. But if it is true that we are not what we should be, it is also true that we are not what we once were. The great work of transformation has already begun in our lives, and though we may not feel especially glorious, it should encourage us that God already sees in us some resemblance to His Son, and while we do well to grieve over the slightness of that resemblance, we should rejoice that it makes us glorious, and go on 'being confident of this very thing, that He which hath begun a good work in you will perform it until the day of Jesus Christ' (Phil. 1:6)

THE CATALYST OF THE CHANGE

2 Corinthians 3:18 tells us about the present progress of glorification that God is carrying out in the lives of His people. It also tells us what produces this change, what is its catalyst. It is the act of 'beholding ... the glory of the

Lord' that causes us to grow like Him. Our transformation is supernatural, but it is not mystical. It is the contemplation of Christ, as recorded for us in Scripture, that will mould and shape our lives, causing us to manifest ever more of His character and glory. As always, the path to spiritual growth is through the Word of God, and there are no shortcuts.

THE CONSUMMATION OF THE CHANGE

Beholding Christ in Scripture is the catalyst of the great change that God intends for His people. It is the sight of Christ Himself that will perfect and complete this change. 'We know that, when He shall appear, we shall be like Him; for we shall see Him as He is' (1 Jn 3:2). In that moment, as we look, for the first time, on our Saviour and our Lord, we will be fashioned like Him. Suddenly, the work of transformation, so gradual, so slow, will have its perfect completion.

What it will be to experience the reality of this change beggars our imagination. Even the apostle who knew his Lord so intimately cannot scale the heights of God's purpose for His own. 'It doth not yet appear what we shall be', but it is enough for John, and enough for us, to know that we will be like Him: all our imperfections and frailties erased and obliterated, never to be grieved by our sinfulness, never to mourn our failure, equipped, for all Eternity, to glorify and to enjoy our blessed Saviour and Lord.

CHAPTER SIX

THE JUDGEMENT SEAT OF CHRIST

FROM BEGINNING TO END, Scripture is packed with promises. Both the first and the last of these promises speak of the coming of Christ. In Genesis 3, it is His first coming to bruise the serpent's head (Gen. 3:15) that is in view. In the closing chapter of the Bible, His return for His own is promised three times over. Both the imminence and the implications of this glorious event are stressed. The Saviour three times promises 'I come quickly' (Rev. 22:7, 12, 20), and on each occasion the verb is in the present tense. 'Behold I am coming quickly' says the Lord Jesus, 'Surely I am coming quickly.'

At the close of a book that speaks of cataclysmic judgement, this threefold promise is a powerful consolation. But with its consolation comes a challenge, for the return of Christ has important implications for every believer: 'My reward is with Me, to give every man according as his work shall be' (v. 12). The Saviour is coming back not just to rapture and rescue His own, but to review and reward their service. The Rapture will mark the commencement of two parallel series of events.

On earth, the day of the Lord will begin, and the horrors of the Tribulation will fall upon the nations. At the same time, in the heavenly sphere, the day of Christ will begin. In contrast to the day of the Lord, it will be a time of glorification and rejoicing, but it begins with the evaluation of the service of each believer.

This event is described in Romans 14:10 and 2 Corinthians 5:10 as 'the judgement seat of Christ', and in both these passages the term 'judgement seat' translates the Greek word *bema*. At the time Paul wrote, the term had come to be used for the raised official seat on which a magistrate or judge sat, but its original use referred to the raised platform where officials at the Greek games presided and where prizes were awarded, and Paul's fondness for using sporting contests as a metaphor for the Christian life suggests that it is this aspect of the term that is especially in view.*

Revelation 22:12 indicates that the review of our service is personal. It is personal, first of all, for it is Christ Who will judge. 'I come quickly, ... My reward is with Me.' The same truth is emphasised by the fact that both references to the *bema* describe it as 'the judgement seat of Christ'. Romans 14:4 explains the importance of this: 'Who art thou that judgest another man's servant? To his own master he standeth or falleth.' Every believer is Christ's servant, and this should make us very cautious about attempting to assess the service of others. But it is also important that we remember that our service is for Christ. We cannot be carelessly dismissive of the input and advice of other believers, but ultimately we do not answer to them, but to Christ. To serve for the plaudits of men is wrong, so is a failure to serve lest we suffer criticism. Christ has redeemed us that we might serve Him and our only concern should be that He is

---

* See, for example, 1 Cor. 9:24–26 Phil. 2:16, Gal. 2:2; 5:7, and 2 Tim. 2:5; 4:7.

satisfied with that service. This should be the priority of our lives, as it was of the apostle's: 'But with me it is a very small thing that I should be judged of you, or of man's judgement: yea, I judge not mine own self. For I know nothing by myself; yet am I not hereby justified: but he that judgeth me is the Lord.' (1 Cor. 4:3–4).

The review at the judgement seat is also personal in the sense that it will affect each believer. No one will be exempt – 'we must all appear before the judgement seat of Christ' (2 Cor. 5:10). Service for God is not an optional extra, limited to a select cadre of believers. It is the privilege, as well as the responsibility, of every Christian. And God notes all service, however humble it may seem to us, and will ensure that all that is done for Him, in accordance with His will, shall have its reward.

The probing investigation of the *bema* will focus on our service – 'to give every man according as his work shall be'. Our sins will not be in question. Christ has borne the punishment that they deserved, and on the basis of His work, God has promised that our sins and our iniquities 'will [He] remember no more' (Heb. 8:12). But our work for Christ will be thoroughly tested.

The quality of our service will be tested. 'Every man's work shall be made manifest: for the day shall declare it, because it shall be revealed by fire; and the fire shall try every man's work of what sort it is' (1 Cor. 3:13). Gold, silver, and precious stones will retain their value in this test. That which was costly, that required careful effort and laborious mining will prove its enduring worth. That which was simple bulk, which cost little, and lay convenient to hand, will vanish, meriting no reward.

Our faithfulness to God's Word will be tested. 1 Corinthians 3 demonstrates that service of lasting value must be built on the only valid foundation, and must contribute to the growth and development of the local assembly. Energy and effort expended in other spheres find no mention here. Similarly, 2 Timothy 2:5 reminds us that ' if a man also strive for masteries, yet is he not crowned, except he strive lawfully'. The solemn reality is that God will only reward service that is in accordance with His will. If I wish to ensure that the sacrifice of my time, skills and abilities will result in eternal reward, I would do well to pour my endeavour into the work of the assembly, and not dissipate it in efforts that do not enjoy scriptural sanction.

The motives behind our service will also be laid bare as Christ 'will bring to light the hidden things of darkness, and will make manifest the counsels of the hearts' (1 Cor. 4:5). This is a searching thought. How often do we do the right thing for the wrong reason? At times we can scarcely account for our own motives, and it is folly to try to judge the motives of others. In that day, all this will be laid bare, and Christ's evaluation will be incontestable in its accuracy.

This evaluation will have one of two results. The first possibility is that the believer could 'suffer loss' (1 Cor. 3:15). What a solemn thing it will be to see a whole life go up in flames, to realise that we have wasted our time, our gifts, and our talents, and to find ourselves standing before Christ, with hands that are empty, because we never took care to fill them. But for all that endures there will be reward. Scripture speaks of the crowns that will be given – for self-discipline (1 Cor. 9:25), stewardship and loving His appearing (2 Tim. 4:7–8), shepherding (1 Pet. 5:4), soul-winning (Phil. 4:1; 1 Thess. 2:19), and enduring temptation and tribulation (Jas 1:12; Rev. 2:10). What joy it will be to receive an incorruptible crown from the nail-pierced hands of our Saviour, and to hear 'well done, thou good and faithful servant' (Mt. 25:21). And what an inexpressible privilege it will be to take whatever crowns we have been able by God's grace to win, and to cast them at our Saviour's feet, confessing 'Thou art worthy, O Lord' (Rev. 4:11). What sacrifice will then seem too great, what service too demanding? May God give us grace to live in the light of that day, and to serve Him 'acceptably with reverence and godly fear' (Heb. 12:28).

Chapter Seven

The Marriage of the Lamb

A BEAUTIFUL YOUNG WOMAN, mounted on a camel, moved slowly through the wastes of the Negev desert. As the reddening sky darkened over the shimmering sands, she listened with rapt attention to the words of the servant who travelled at her side. Throughout her entire days-old acquaintance with this man, he had spoken of only one subject. And yet the subject had lost nothing of its charm. Far from being bored, the girl longed to hear more of the man whom she had never yet met, and who had still managed to woo and win her heart.

But the servant seemed less talkative now. A newly electric feeling of tension, of expectation, filled the air as again and again he broke off his discourse to scan the horizon, till, at last, with a sudden exclamation he directed Rebekah's gaze to Isaac's lone figure. Hastily she dismounted from her camel and, carefully adjusting her veil, waited breathlessly to meet her bridegroom. Both Isaac and Rebekah had longed for that meeting, but it was only the beginning, a prelude to a marriage, and to a lifetime of mutual comfort and communion. 'Isaac brought her into his mother Sarah's tent, and took Rebekah, and she became his wife; and he loved her'

(Gen. 24:67), the first mention in Scripture of love between a husband and his wife.

The story of Isaac and Rebekah is one of the great romances of Scripture. It is, however, more than just a sweet story. Rebekah's experience provides us with a beautiful illustration of the Church. Like Rebekah, we have been called to be the bride of a Man 'Whom having not seen we love', and are making our way through the wilderness, learning more of Him through the self-effacing ministry of the Holy Spirit, and longing for the first sight of the One Who 'comes to meet us on our desert way'. Like Rebekah, we should long for that meeting with every fibre of our being. But we too should remember that the meeting we anticipate so eagerly will be only the beginning. It too will be followed by the confirmation and consummation of eternal communion – the marriage of the Lamb.

For all its tenderness, the tale of Isaac and Rebekah is but a faint intimation of this glorious event. The Church stands at the pinnacle of God's dealings with mankind, and the marriage of the Lamb marks the zenith of His designs for the Church. The Saviour's great intention for His Church is 'that He might present it to Himself a glorious church, not having spot, or wrinkle, or any such thing; but that it should be holy and without blemish' (Eph. 5:27). His love and His sacrifice have alike been directed to this great end. His eternal purpose for His bride will finally arrive at its consummation, and she will be united with Him, as a meet companion, uniquely fitted to be 'the fulness of Him that filleth all in all' (Eph. 1:23).

Scripture does not give us a precise time point for this glorious event. However, it is clear that it takes place before Christ's return in glorious manifestation. Revelation 19:7 states that 'the marriage ['wedding celebration', NET] of the Lamb is come, and His wife hath made herself ready'. The tense of 'is come' demonstrates that this is an event that is already complete, a point that is confirmed by the fact that the Church is now described as Christ's wife. This declaration forms part of the prelude to the opening of the heavens, and the riding forth of the conquering Christ (v. 11 ff.). Revelation 19:7, therefore, gives us an endpoint, before which the marriage must take place. Verse 8 of the same chapter gives us a start point. It describes the Church as 'arrayed in fine linen ... [which] is the righteousness of the saints.' 'Righteousness' is plural in this verse, and the idea here is 'acts of the saints that have been declared righteousness'. That declaration will take place as part of the judgement of believers' service at the *bema* of Christ.

The marriage of the Lamb, then, will take place somewhere in the period between the judgement seat and the manifestation of Christ. To say more than this is speculation, but it hardly seems likely that too long a gap will intervene between the *bema* and the marriage. It would be a strange bridegroom who wished his wedding postponed, and even the most ardent earthly love pales by comparison with the love – and the longing – of Christ for His bride.

The timing of the event also establishes its location. Isaac's marriage to Rebekah took place after he had received her into his mother's tent. Our union to Christ will be perfected after He has received us into His Father's house (Jn 14:3). It will be a heavenly ceremony, and an intimate one and in its love and joy will stand in stark contrast to the dreadful Tribulation events that will be unfolding on earth.

But the joy of the Lamb and His bride will not be constrained to the heavenly sphere, or limited to the time span between the *bema* and Christ's glorious manifestation. The custom of Jewish marriages at the time of Christ was for the marriage ceremony to be followed by a marriage feast that would last for days, and to which a great number of friends and relations would be invited. It was a feast of this sort that the Lord Jesus attended in Cana of Galilee (Jn 2) and that was the subject of the parable He told in Matthew 22.

Matthew 22 is one of the passages that describes the event referred in Revelation 19:9 as 'the marriage supper of the Lamb'. In contrast to the heavenly intimacy of the marriage ceremony, this feast is earthly and public. The whole millennial reign of Christ with its blessing and its bounty will be the feast at which this marriage is celebrated. The parables of Matthew 22 and 25 furnish part of the guest list. Those who have heeded the gospel of the kingdom, who have prepared for the arrival of the Bridegroom, and who will enter the Millennium will enjoy the great feast. In addition, saints of past dispensations, now in resurrection bodies, will gather at the feast, as 'friends' of the Bridegroom (Jn 3:29).

It is God's intention 'that in the ages to come He might shew the exceeding riches of His grace in His kindness toward us through Christ Jesus' (Eph. 2:7). As she appears with Him in all the glory of her bridal garments, the wonder of what His grace has done in calling, and cleansing, and perfecting the ruined wrecks of sin will be evident to all. As she sits with Him in the place of honour at the marriage feast, all creation will learn afresh of the astounding accomplishment of Divine grace. And amidst it all, we will enjoy a perfect closeness, intimacy, and communion that will grow yet more perfect as the ages of eternity roll.

Surely the anticipation of this event should fill and thrill our souls. Like Rebekah, we should long to learn more of the Bridegroom Who so soon 'will come to meet us on the desert way.' And as we think of the day when we will appear with Him in glory, clothed in fine linen, let us resolve, by our service for Him, to embroider and embellish our wedding garment that we may eternally have the capacity to fittingly portray His infinite glory.

Chapter Eight

IN THE THRONE ROOM OF ETERNITY

Revelation 4 and 5 record some of the most remarkable scenes in Scripture. Their scale and significance are alike vast, and they defy any attempt to deal with them at all comprehensively in the scope of a short chapter like this. Nonetheless, as we are privileged to share John's perspective on this majestic scene, there are a number of important points that we must notice.

We should consider first the prelude to the scene. The first three chapters of Revelation have been occupied with 'the things which are' (Rev. 1:19). In particular, they have been concerned with assembly testimony. Many commentators have seen in the seven churches an outline of the history of the Church age. Whether or not we subscribe to this view, we can readily agree that the conditions and challenges of assembly testimony are addressed in each of the seven letters. At the conclusion of this section, John is called up to heaven, away from an increasingly troubled earth, to enjoy a unique perspective on the events that are about to take place. This heavenly summons provides us with a lovely picture of the Rapture, which will bring to an end the earthly testimony of the Church and will usher in the events that begin to unfold in Revelation 4 and 5.

Having been transported to heaven, John found himself viewing a remarkable prospect. The splendour, colour, and radiance of the scene described beggar our imagination. The glowing lamps, the rainbow and the sea of glass, the motions of beasts and elders, and the glory of angelic myriads, of white robes, of glittering diadems and of golden vials, and the flashings of the lightning would be more than sufficient to dazzle the eye and to daze the senses. But all this radiance is just a frame, reflecting and refracting the all-surpassing glory of the One Who sits on heaven's throne.

Around this throne, are grouped the participants in these scenes of glory. The symbolism of these participants has not always been the subject of unanimous agreement. The four beasts, or living creatures, seem to be representative of created life in all its aspects. They give 'glory and honour and thanks to Him that sat on the throne' (Rev. 4:9), and their praise prompts the twenty-four elders to acknowledge 'Thou hast created all things, and for Thy pleasure they are and were created' (Rev. 4:11).

In the case of the twenty-four elders there are a number of elements that allow us to conclude that they are linked with the Church. Firstly, their name is significant. They are described as elders, or seniors, a term whose meaning would be difficult to comprehend if they were angelic beings, and thus deathless and ageless. Their attire, too, is important. Both the white garments and the diadems that they wear are symbolic of rewarded service, and elsewhere in Scripture are linked with believers of the present dispensation. Thirdly, we should note their priestly character. This is emphasised by their number, echoing the courses of the Levitical priesthood, and by their actions, as they pour out the golden vials, filled with the prayers of the saints, before the throne of God. Finally, we should notice their song. In chapter 5, they sing of their redemption to God from every kindred and tongue and people and nation, and of the blessings into which they have been brought, in language uniquely befitting those who have been saved in this age, and made part of the royal priesthood (1 Pet. 2:9).

As the action of the scene unfolds, our attention is drawn to the parchment, the scroll with the seven seals that is held in the right hand of the One upon the Throne. From its description, and from its presentation in this passage, this scroll has been described as the 'title deeds of earth'. The events that follow the opening of its seals, and the implied unrolling of the scroll, make it clear that it encompasses and documents God's prophetic plan for earth.

John appreciates the importance of this scroll. This is clear from his response to the problem that emerges. A strong angel sends out a challenge – 'Who is worthy to open the book, and to loose the seals thereof?' His question launches a cosmic search through all of creation for one who would be worthy to claim the title deeds and unfold God's prophetic plan. That the search is fruitless reflects the total depravity of humanity. In the Fall, man had lost his position as Creation's head. The rights that God had delegated to him were lost when Adam sinned. Now, as the human race in its entirety is searched, not a single individual is found worthy to take the scroll and to open its seals. The problem, and its implications have a profound impact upon John. As God's purposes for creation seem to have been thwarted by man's failure, he weeps much. His grief was deep – this is the word used of Rachel's weeping for her children (Mt. 2:18), of Peter's tears of repentance (Mt. 26:75), and of the Saviour's lament over Jerusalem (Lk. 19:41). But his grief is assuaged by the words of the elder, and by the realization that, in spite of human failure, there is one glorious Person Who has the right to take the scroll from the right hand of the Throne-sitter.

Notwithstanding their striking description and remarkable significance, the beasts and the elders, along with the accompanying myriads of angels, are only attendants. At this crucial moment of the action, John's attention is turned to the 'Lion of the tribe of Juda, the Root of David' (5:5). John looks for this formidable being, and beholds, in the midst of the throne, a slain, yet living Lamb. It is the risen Lord Jesus Christ Who is at the centre of this majestic scene. His unique authority is demonstrated as He takes the scroll from the right hand of God.

John's tears are turned to triumph as the Lamb receives the scroll. In the chapters that follow he will witness as the seals are broken, and the scroll is unrolled, unfolding God's great prophetic programme. Three series of judgements are described – the seven seals, the seven trumpets, and the seven vials. These Divine judgements are poured out upon a rebellious earth with awful and escalating severity. As they proceed, John is granted a heavenly view of the events of the Tribulation. These will unfold on earth, where all will be confusion and turmoil. From the privileged perspective of heaven's throne room, however, the inexorable order of God's programme will be evident.

In light of this, we can scarcely wonder at the praise that marks these scenes. Indeed, if we rightly appreciate the import of the events that John recalls, we cannot but join the swelling song of worship that resounds through heaven. In chapter 4, the beasts and elders proclaimed before the throne the praises of the Creator (v. 9, 11). Now, the beasts and the four and twenty elders break forth into a new song, declaring 'Thou art worthy ... for Thou wast slain, and hast redeemed us to God' (v. 9). They do not sing alone, for their praise spreads farther and farther, until the whole cosmos is united in the re-echoing exaltation of the Lamb that is worthy. Revelation 5 ends with a mighty tumult of praise to God and to Christ. We cannot read the words without taking up the strain, as worship awakens in our hearts. How wonderful it will be, in that coming day, not just to echo the song, but to be the leaders of heaven's praise and worship of the Lion of the tribe of Juda, the slain and living Lamb, Who is exclusively and uniquely worthy of blessing, and honour, and glory, and power.

Chapter Nine

THE COMMENCEMENT OF THE TRIBULATION

THE ASSEMBLY AT THESSALONICA was in turmoil. They were enduring 'persecutions and tribulations' (2 Thess. 1:4), passing through a time of intense pressure and suffering. But though these circumstances were taxing, they were not, in themselves, the greatest disturbance to the peace of the Thessalonian believers. A more devastating threat came from those who sought to interpret and explain the Thessalonians' sufferings. Claiming apostolic authority for their teaching, these propagators of false doctrine pointed to the prevailing conditions as proof positive 'that the day of the Lord is present' (2 Thess. 2:2, JND). The trials through which the believers were passing, they suggested, demonstrated that the Tribulation had begun.

The Thessalonian believers should, of course, have known better than to give credence to this teaching. After all, in the first epistle, Paul had singled out their expectation of Christ's return, and their salvation from the Tribulation as one of the outstanding features of their testimony: 'ye turned to God from idols to serve a living and true God, and to await His Son from the heavens, whom He raised from among the dead, Jesus, our deliverer from the coming wrath (1 Thess. 1:9–10, JND). Later in the first epistle, Paul urged the believers to put on 'for an helmet, the hope of salvation. For God hath not appointed us to wrath, but to obtain salvation by our Lord Jesus Christ' (1 Thess. 5:8–9). This knowledge that God had marked them out, not to pass through the ravages of the Tribulation, but to obtain salvation, ought to have stayed and steadied their thoughts, and armoured their minds against the assault of false teaching.

But, as ever, it was one thing to know the truth in theory, and quite another to keep hold of it in the midst of trial and turmoil, and with the specious arguments and explanations of the apostles of error hammering on their ears. Paul understood this, and feared that these believers would be 'shaken in mind, or be troubled' (2 Thess. 2:2). And so he writes to reassure them by reminding them of the things he had told them while he was with them (2:5) about the events that would take place before and during the Tribulation.

He begins by taking them back to the truth that had been so central to the first epistle. As the Thessalonians looked with dismay at the events that were unfolding about them, and began to entertain the idea that something had gone wrong and that they were, after all, in the day of the Lord, Paul hastens to remind them of the truth that would, more than any other, restore and reinforce their peace of mind. So, he beseeches them 'by the coming of our Lord Jesus Christ, and by our gathering together unto Him' (2:1). That Christ was coming was a comfort, but the reminder that, at His coming, they were going – leaving earth to be gathered to Him 'in the air' (1 Thess. 4:17) – went right to the heart of the Thessalonians' fears.

Paul adds to that comfort in the following verses by outlining two events that must take place before the day of the Lord could begin. These events are firstly, 'the falling away' (2 Thess. 2:3) and secondly, the revelation (the apocalypse, or unveiling) of the man of sin (vv. 3–4). 'Falling away' is 'apostasy', a word that means 'departure', or even 'rebellion'. Some commentators have understood this in a spatial sense and have seen in this verse another reference to the Rapture. However, its usage elsewhere in Scripture and in other texts supports the more traditional view that the text refers to a great spiritual and religious departure.* The history of Christendom has been marked by much apostasy – denial of and departure from Divine truth. This, however, is *the* apostasy, an act of rejection unique in its significance. This remarkable apostasy will set the stage for the revelation of the man of sin ['lawlessness', ESV] 'the son of perdition. Who opposeth and exalteth himself above all that is called God, or that is worshipped; so that he as God sitteth in the temple of God, shewing himself that he is God.' So thoroughly will Christendom have turned from God that the vaunting claims of this usurper will be accepted, and his self-enthronement will be accepted and applauded by those who have utterly and finally departed from any glimmering of the truth.

The fact that the day of the Lord could not begin before these events took place must surely have reassured the Thessalonians, as it should us. But another question would have arisen in their minds. Granted, the apostasy had not taken place when Paul wrote, but was it possible that they would soon see this full-blown apostasy and find themselves in the Tribulation?

---

* See, for a helpful consideration of this issue, William W. Combs, 'Is *Apostasia* in 2 Thessalonians 2:3 a Reference to the Rapture?', *Detroit Baptist Seminary Journal*, (1998), 3, pp. 63–87.

Paul addresses this question by going back over the events that he has already covered. But he does not simply rewind and replay. Rather, he moves to a different point of view. Paul takes us behind the scenes of Divine purpose to enable us more clearly to understand why neither the apostasy nor the Antichrist can emerge before the Rapture has taken place:

> And now ye know what withholdeth ['restrains' *JND*], that he might be revealed in his time. For the mystery of iniquity doth already work: only He Who now letteth ['restrains' *JND*] will let, until He be taken out of the way. And then shall that Wicked be revealed (2 Thess. 2:6–8).

The apostasy and the revelation of the man of sin are being restrained. These verses present two restrainers – a 'what' in verse 6, and a 'Who' in verse 7. The restraining person will be 'taken out of the way', and then – and only then – will 'that Wicked' be revealed. While there have been some differences in the interpretation of these verses, the understanding that the Church is in view in verse 6, and the Holy Spirit in verse 7, seems to fit best with the context here. Satan is not free to act as he wills. The presence on earth of the Holy Spirit, indwelling the Church, withholds the fruition and fulfilment of his diabolical designs for earth. Only when the Church is removed at the Rapture, and the Holy Spirit 'taken out of the way', will the final and climactic apostasy take place, and the man of sin be revealed.

The Thessalonian believers, then, did not need to fear that the day of the Lord was present, and that they had entered into the Tribulation. The very fact that they remained on earth indicated that Divine power was still restraining. Not only could the Tribulation not begin while they were still on earth – even the necessary preliminaries could not take place. And so they could face both the assault of circumstances and the attack of error without dismay. At the commencement of the chapter, Paul had expressed his concern that their minds and their emotions would be disturbed – that they would be 'shaken in mind' and 'troubled'. As he brings the chapter to its close, his prayer is that their hearts and minds would alike be reached:

> Now our Lord Jesus Christ Himself, and God, even our Father, which hath loved us, and hath given us everlasting consolation and good hope through grace. Comfort your hearts, and stablish you in every good word and work (vv. 16–17).

May the truth of God's Word, and an understanding of our place in the eternal purposes of God likewise equip us to face the challenges and the errors of our own day.

CHAPTER TEN

THE CHARACTER OF THE TRIBULATION

TWO DAYS BEFORE the end of the earthly ministry of the Lord Jesus Christ, He passed, with His disciples, through the courts of the Temple. He had just delivered an excoriating rebuke to the scribes and Pharisees, closing with the solemn declaration 'ye shall not see Me henceforth, till ye shall say, "Blessed is He that cometh in the name of the Lord"' (Mt. 23:39). Now, as He left the Temple courts for the last time, the disciples, motivated perhaps by glorious visions of a day of recognition, drew His attention to the splendour of the buildings. This, they must have assumed, would be the place where the Messiah would be acknowledged by the nation. Surely these courts would soon echo with the acclaim of a people who had finally come to share Peter's recognition that here was 'the Christ, the Son of the living God' (Mt. 16:16). But all their expectations were overturned by the blunt clarity of the Saviour's response: 'See ye not all these things? Verily I say unto you, There shall not be left here one stone upon another, that shall not be thrown down' (Mt. 24:2).

It is not difficult to imagine the confusion and consternation that filled the disciples' minds as they made their way, in an awkward silence, towards the Mount of Olives. Eventually, their desire for clarification spilled over into speech. Approaching the Lord Who always dealt so patiently with their questions and queries they asked 'Tell us, when shall these things be? and what shall be the sign of Thy coming, and of the end of the world?' (v. 3). And they did not question in vain. In response to their anxious query, the Lord Jesus delivered to them a revelation of crucial importance, an unveiling of prophetic truth sometimes known as the 'little apocalypse'.

THE PERIODS OF THE TRIBULATION

In this discourse, the Saviour spoke of two periods of global turmoil. The first, outlined in verses 5–14, will be marked by national conflict and natural calamities: 'nation shall rise against nation, and kingdom against kingdom: and there shall be famines, and pestilences, and earthquakes, in divers places' (v. 7). This period is described as the 'beginning of sorrows' (v. 8). The end of this period is marked by a prodigious occurrence, when men would see 'the abomination of desolation, spoken of by Daniel the prophet, stand in the holy place' (v. 15). This event will be followed by a period of intensified trouble, chillingly described by the Lord Jesus as 'great tribulation, such as was not since the beginning of the world to this time, no, nor ever shall be' (v. 21). This period of unparalleled affliction will be so extensive in its scale and so appalling in its severity as to surpass all the horrors of history. Then, 'immediately after the tribulation of those days' the darkening of the sun and the moon, and the shaking of the heavens would signal the event that was central to the disciples' question – 'the Son of man coming in the clouds of heaven with power and great glory' (vv. 29–30).

The Saviour had made explicit reference to 'Daniel the prophet', but even had He not done so, the minds of the disciples would surely have gone to Daniel 9, and to the prophecy of the last of Daniel's seventy weeks: 'And he [the prince that shall come] shall confirm the covenant with many for one week: and in the midst of the week he shall cause the sacrifice and the oblation to cease, and for the overspreading of abominations he shall make it desolate, even until the consummation, and that determined shall be poured upon the desolate' (Dan. 9:27). This passage provides us with the timeframe of the events outlined in Matthew 24. The seven years of this last week (often known as the Tribulation, or the day of the Lord) will be divided by the setting up of the abomination of desolation into two equal three-and-a-half year periods – the beginning of sorrows and the Great Tribulation, also known as 'the time of Jacob's trouble' (Jer. 30:7).

THE PEOPLE OF THE TRIBULATION

The Tribulation will be marked by dramatic and devastating events. Involved in these events will be a number of significant figures. The first of these we have already encountered in the previous chapter. He is the 'prince that shall come' of Daniel 9, the 'man of sin', the 'lawless one' of 2 Thessalonians 2:8 (*JND*), and the 'first beast' of Revelation 11, 13, and 18. 2 Thessalonians 2 tells us a little about the character and actions of this man. He is characterised by lawlessness. Uniquely, he shares with Judas the title 'son of perdition'. And his aim is total opposition to God, or to all that is called God. Other passages of Scripture will fill in the details of this evil figure. From a comparison of Revelation 13:1 and Revelation 17:15, we learn that he is a Gentile. He is the leader of a revived Roman empire (Dan. 9:26). He leads a great political and military federation (Rev. 13:1; 17:12–14) based on diplomacy (Dan. 8:24–5; Rev. 17:12) and on conquest (Dan. 7:8, 24). He will be a man of remarkable ability (Dan. 7:8, 20; 8:23–5) and of great guile (Ezek. 28:2–5). Ultimately, the source of his power and the energy behind his meteoric rise to global prominence and dominance is satanic (Rev. 13:4; 2 Thess. 2:9). He will be hailed and acknowledged by those 'who received not the love of the truth that they might be saved' (2 Thess. 2:10). Having rejected the truth of the gospel, these individuals will be judicially blinded – God will 'send them strong delusion, that they should believe a lie' (v. 11). This man's abilities will be immense, and his ascent of the ladder of earthly power unstoppable, but behind it all will be working the power of Satan.

This man will be joined by another figure – the second beast of Revelation 13, who is also described as the false prophet (Rev. 16:13; 19:20; 20:10). While the first beast rises from the sea – the symbol of the Gentile nations – the second beast rises from the land. He will a Jew, and will lead the apostate religion that will emerge after the Rapture. He will have the power to perform lying miracles. At the end of the first half of the Tribulation, he will give life to the image of the beast and 'and cause that as many as would not worship the image of the beast should be killed' (Rev. 13:15).

As the Tribulation unfolds, these evil figures will stride the world stage. Their political, religious and social dominion will be all but absolute. But Satan's triumph will not be complete, for in this, as in every age, God has preserved a remnant for and testimony to Himself. The first element of this testimony will be the ministry of the two witnesses outlined in Revelation 11. These men will stand in the street of Jerusalem clothed in sackcloth. Under direct Divine protection they will testify for 1,260 days (or three-and-a-half years) until they have 'finished their testimony' and are put to death by the beast, only to rise after three and a half days, and ascend to heaven. Some debate exists as to the identity of these witnesses – are they two literal figures, or is two simply symbolic of witness? Are they actually or symbolically Moses and Elijah? Similarly, there is disagreement as to the period of their ministry. It seems likely, however, that they are two literal individuals who will testify for the first half of the Tribulation, a solemn voice of warning that will be disregarded by the great majority of mankind.

These witnesses will not be alone in their testimony. Revelation 7 describes the sealing of 144,000 witnesses, drawn from the twelve tribes of Israel, who will go forth during the Tribulation with a worldwide mission to preach the gospel of the kingdom. These Jewish witnesses will have trusted Christ after the Rapture, and their ministry will be directed to those in every part of the globe who have not previously rejected the gospel message (2 Thess. 2:10). Under Divine protection, and in the face of intense persecution they go forth to preach. And their ministry will prosper. The fruits of their preaching will be 'a great multitude, which no man could number, of all nations, and kindreds, and people, and tongues' (Rev. 7:9) who 'have washed their robes, and made them white in the blood of the Lamb' (Rev. 7:14). Even as evil ranges rampant through the globe God will be at work, saving souls and preparing a vast multitude to enter the blessings of the millennial kingdom.

These are some of the people who will be involved in the Tribulation. But let us not forget that there is one group who will not experience anything of its turmoil and suffering. How blessed it is to know that we who have trusted Christ have not been appointed to wrath, but 'to obtain salvation by our Lord Jesus Christ' (1

Thess. 5:9). Reader, where do you stand? If it should be that you have never trusted Christ, let the truths that we have considered be a solemn voice of warning. 'Flee from the wrath to come' (Lk. 3:7).

Chapter Eleven

The Course of the Tribulation

As we have already seen, 1 Thessalonians 4:15–18 provide us with Scripture's most comprehensive overview of the Rapture. At the close of the section, Paul urges his readers to 'comfort one another' with this glorious and imminent hope. In the verses that follow, Paul looks at the same event from an alternative perspective. For believers, the Rapture is a blessed and comforting hope, for the unsaved, it is something altogether different: 'For yourselves know perfectly that the day of the Lord so cometh as a thief in the night. For when they shall say, Peace and safety; then sudden destruction cometh upon them, as travail upon a woman with child; and they shall not escape' (1 Thess. 5:2–3). The Tribulation will not begin at the moment of the Rapture, but the return of Christ and the removal of the saints will be a signal that God's prophetic programme is once again in motion, and that the day of the Lord – the Tribulation – is beginning, that trouble will come suddenly and with increasing intensity.

The storm will break out of a clear sky. No doubt the Rapture of the saints will occasion much stir and speculation, but it will not leave any lasting mark on the thoughts of men. They will enjoy 'peace and security' (1 Thess. 5:3, *ESV*). This sense of safety is not difficult to understand. As we have seen in previous chapters, one of the things that will mark the commencement of Daniel's seventieth week is the making of a covenant between the beast – and the global superpower that he leads – and the nation of Israel. At a stroke the most intractable geopolitical problem of modern times will be solved. The Middle Eastern question, the source of so much war, violence, and terror, will appear to be definitively answered. The world will breathe a sigh of relief and relax. And then, suddenly, terrifyingly, destruction will fall.

For those who are on earth, the events of Daniel's seventieth week will be traumatic beyond our imaginings. The faithful remnant will turn to prophetic Scripture, and find in it the reassurance that all is in God's hands, but for the majority, the period will be one of terror and astonishment.

As we have seen, the first half of the Tribulation is the 'beginning of sorrows', a period of war, famine, and pestilence. These events are outlined in Revelation 6–11. In these chapters, the opening of the seven seals, and the sounding of the seven trumpets usher in the escalating judgements that will be experienced by those on earth. The seal judgements of Revelation 6–8 closely follow the description laid out by the Lord Jesus – wars (Rev. 6:3–4), famine (vv. 5–6), pestilence (vv. 7–8), and earthquakes (Rev. 8:1–6). These are followed by the trumpet judgements, which grow increasingly severe and extensive, until 'the days of the voice of the seventh angel, when he shall begin to sound, the mystery of God should be finished, as He hath declared to His servants the prophets' (Rev. 10:7).

At this halfway point in Daniel's seventieth week a number of important events take place. Satan and his angels are cast down to earth in 'great wrath, because he knoweth that he hath but a short time' (Rev. 12:9–12). This will signal a dramatic intensification in the Tribulation.

At this point, too, the abomination of desolation will be set up. To discover what this will involve, we need to compare the words of Matthew 24:15 and Mark 13:14, with those of 2 Thessalonians 2:4. The Lord Jesus foretold that the abomination of desolation would 'stand in the holy place', 'where it ought not'. The apostle Paul describes how the man of sin 'opposeth and exalteth himself above all that is called God, or that is worshipped; so that he as God sitteth in the temple of God, shewing himself that he is God.' Along with these passages we can consider Revelation 13:14–15, where the false prophet 'deceiveth them that dwell on the earth by the means of those miracles which he had power to do in the sight of the beast; saying to them that dwell on the earth, that they should make an image to the beast... And he had power to give life unto the image of the beast, that the image of the beast should both speak, and cause that as many as would not worship the image of the beast should be killed.' Taken together, these Scriptures indicate that the second beast, the false prophet, will cause the image of the first beast to be set up in the Temple, positioned in the holy of holies as the only permissible object of worship. It is this event that will signal the breaking of his covenant, the cessation of the continual burnt offering, and the commencement of his persecution of the godly Jewish remnant, which will refuse to pay him the homage he demands. This will be the triumphant climax of Satan's great counterfeit of Christianity, a corrupt religious system described in

Revelation 17 and 18 as 'Babylon the great, the mother of harlots and abominations of the earth'.

To enforce this universal worship, the beast will introduce a visible sign – and test – of loyalty. He will require 'all, both small and great, rich and poor, free and bond, to receive a mark in their right hand, or in their foreheads: And that no man might buy or sell, save he that had the mark, or the name of the beast, or the number of his name' (Rev. 13:16–17).

The abomination of desolation will signal the commencement of the time of Jacob's Trouble, and from this point, satanic persecution of the faithful Jewish remnant will intensify. As foretold by the Lord Jesus in Matthew 24:16–20, these faithful Jews find their only hope of survival in fleeing 'into the wilderness' (Rev. 12:6) where they will be 'nourished for a time, and times, and half a time [i.e. three-and-a-half years], from the face of the serpent' (v. 14).

The Great Tribulation will be a time of unprecedented military, political, and economic upheaval – it will be 'a time of trouble, such as never was since there was a nation' (Dan. 12:1). From the perspective of human history, the actions and endeavours of men will be unparalleled in their scope and scale. But Psalm 2 gives us a very different view of their value:

> Why do the heathen rage, and the people imagine a vain thing? The kings of the earth set themselves, and the rulers take counsel together, against the LORD, and against His anointed, saying, Let us break Their bands asunder, and cast away Their cords from us (vv. 1–3).

All of their opposition to God and to His purpose will be futile:

He that sitteth in the heavens shall laugh: the LORD shall have them in derision. Then shall He speak unto them in His wrath, and vex them in His sore displeasure. Yet have I set My king upon My holy hill of Zion. (vv. 4–6)

All of the turmoil, the trouble, and the suffering of the Tribulation, the shaking of 'the heavens, and the earth, and the sea, and the dry land' and 'all nations' (Hag. 2:6–7) are the demonstration of the righteousness of God, and the redemptive rights of the risen, victorious Son of God. As we see the scroll unfurl in the omnipotent hand of the Lamb, we will be privileged to see the order of unfolding events. Even as men in the throes of the Tribulation will spew out terrible cursings and awful execrations (Rev. 16:11), we will join the song and swell the strains of the song of Moses and of the Lamb:

> Great and marvellous are Thy works, Lord God Almighty; just and true are Thy ways, Thou King of saints. Who shall not fear Thee, O Lord, and glorify Thy name? For Thou only art holy: for all nations shall come and worship before Thee; for Thy judgements are made manifest (Rev. 15:3–4).

And as men will cry to the rocks to hide them 'from the face of Him that sitteth on the throne, and from the wrath of the Lamb' (Rev. 6:16), we will behold His face in righteousness (Ps. 17:15). Well may we sing 'Happy people, happy people, what a Saviour we have found'!

Chapter Twelve

Towards Armageddon

THE TWENTIETH CENTURY fundamentally altered the way in which we look at the earth. The space race allowed man, for the first time, to stand outside of earth and to look down at the planet. Since then, satellite photography and GPS have continued to transform our view of the planet. Notwithstanding the progress of technology, though, there is still something peculiarly fascinating about old maps. And the older they are, the more fascination they hold. Looking at maps that are centuries old allows us to understand something of the way in which long dead generations saw the world. To us, these maps look peculiar – whole countries are missing, and those that do appear are often very oddly shaped. But there are two features of medieval maps, in particular, that would be worthy of imitation by modern cartographers. These maps often depict the eye of God looking down on the world, a reminder that God is interested in all that goes on here on earth. And at the centre of the map they place the city of Jerusalem.

There was, of course, geographical justification for the decision to place Jerusalem at the centre of the world. Jerusalem stands where east meets west, at the junction of Europe, Asia, and Africa, and at the intersection of the great trading routes of the ancient world.

Throughout history, she has been the focus of momentous events.

The sensible reader of Scripture, though, will know that Jerusalem has more than a geographic significance. She is 'the city of the great King' (Ps. 48:2), specially chosen by God, and the focal point of His earthly dealings with mankind. Throughout history and prophecy alike, she has had a special place in His purpose.

During the present dispensation, God's dealings with the nation are providential, rather than prophetic. She has been set aside, until the fulness of the Gentiles has been brought in (Rom. 11:25). But 'the gifts and calling of God are without repentance' (Rom. 11:29), and He still has a purpose for His earthly people. Israel's enduring importance is confirmed in the words of the angel Gabriel to Daniel. The great prophetic outline that Daniel received highlighted the importance not just of the Jewish nation, but also of the city: 'seventy weeks are determined upon thy people and upon thy holy city' (Dan. 9:24).

The prophetic centrality of Israel is emphasised by the way in which Scripture labels the nations whose military might and territorial ambition will be so significant during the Tribulation. We have already encountered the man of sin, who will be the leader of a western power of unprecedented military and economic strength. The covenant that this man will make with Israel, and the close relationship that he will have with the apostate Jewish leader, the false prophet, will be important features of this man's foreign policy. But he will not have the world stage wholly to himself. Scripture tells us that three other military powers will occupy the world stage during the days of the Tribulation. As they are introduced to us in prophetic Scripture, each is identified by its geographical relationship to Israel.

The first of these powers is described as 'Gog, the land of Magog, the chief prince of Meshech and Tubal' (Ezek. 38:2), and its ruler as 'the king of the north' (Dan. 11:40). This king of the north will lead a confederation of nations including Rosh, Meshech, Tubal (Ezek. 38:2, ASV), Gomer, the house of Togarmah, (v. 6) and 'Persia, Cush, and Put (v. 5, ASV). Commentators have offered a range of identifications for these nations, but it is sufficient for our purposes to notice that the confederation comes from the north, and that they band together as a predatory military power.

Ezekiel 38 and 39 describe how this northern power will launch an invasion of the land of Israel. This invasion will take place at a time when the 'people of Israel dwelleth safely' (Ezek. 38:14), which must be the first half of the Tribulation, while she is enjoying the protection furnished by her covenant with the beast. But her peace will be shattered as the northern armies sweep down upon the nation 'as a cloud to cover the land' (v. 16). In this invasion, the king of the north will join with the 'king of the south' (Dan. 11:40). From either end of the land they will come, sweeping over 'the mountains of Israel' (Ezek. 39:2, 3). Their advance will be irresistible. Bound by the terms of his covenant, the beast will scramble to defend Israel, and meet the invading force.

But his strength will not be needed. God will intervene, turning back the armies of the northern power, leaving only a sixth of the original force to retreat in disarray from the land. There will be great seismic convulsions (Ezek. 38:19–20), which will lead to panic and internecine fighting (v. 21), which will be followed by pestilence and 'an overflowing rain, and great hailstones, fire, and brimstone' (v. 22). So catastrophic will the rout of the armies be that it will be seven months before the dead are buried (39:12). Even in the midst of these dark days, God will use the fate of this vast invading force to 'magnify Myself, and sanctify Myself; and I will be known in the eyes of many nations, and they shall know that I am the LORD' (38:23).

Whilst it is clear that the defeat of the invasion is due to the power of God alone, the beast will take full advantage of the opportunity to fill the power vacuum left by the destruction of the armies of the north and south:

> He shall enter also into the glorious land, and many countries shall be overthrown... the land of Egypt shall not escape. But he shall have power over the treasures of gold and of silver, and over all the precious things of Egypt: and the Libyans and the Ethiopians shall be at his steps (Dan. 11:41–43).

The western power of the beast will have overcome the northern and southern powers. But there is still one direction from which trouble can come. Invasion from the east has always been rendered more difficult by the barrier of the Euphrates River. Revelation 9:13–19 describes the build up of a massive army, made up of 'two hundred thousand thousand' horsemen. Up to this point, they have not mobilised. But Revelation 16:12 recounts how 'the sixth angel poured out his vial upon the great river Euphrates; and the water thereof was dried up, that the way of the kings of the east might be prepared.' While the beast is distracted by his great rampage southwards, the kings of the East will launch their offensive. The beast will be stopped in his tracks: 'tidings out of the east and out of the north shall trouble him: therefore he shall go forth with great fury to destroy, and utterly to make away many' (Dan. 11:44). He will gather his troops, and head northwards, moving inexorably towards Armageddon.

We have already seen that the Tribulation will be filled with dramatic and desolating Divine judgements on mankind. Beneath them all, man will still strive for supremacy, armies will scurry to-and-fro, the futile exchange of attack and counter-attack will go wearily on. War is seldom noble, and no war in human history has been as ignoble as the turmoil of the Tribulation. Beyond the fervour of the foot soldiers, the commitment of the generals, and the overweening ambition of the leaders, another force will be at work. In Revelation 16, John describes how he saw 'three unclean spirits like frogs come out of the mouth of the dragon, and out of the mouth of the beast, and out of the mouth of the false prophet. For they are the spirits of devils, working miracles, which go forth unto the kings of the earth and of the whole world, to gather them to the battle of that great day of God Almighty' (Rev. 16:13–14). Satan has always seen men as mere pawns in his long and hopeless campaign against God. The thousands who perish in these conflicts are the cannon fodder of hell.

But another force will be at work, for the eye of God still watches over the world. To the king of the north, He says 'I will turn thee back, and put hooks into thy jaws, and I will bring thee forth, and all thine army, horses and horsemen' (Ezek. 38:4). 'Surely', said the Psalmist, 'the wrath of man shall praise Thee' (Ps. 76:10). True at all times, this principle will operate especially during the Tribulation as, behind the energy, ingenuity, and activity of man, behind the awful malignity of Satan, a sovereign and omnipotent God calmly works His eternal and inexorable purpose out.

CHAPTER THIRTEEN

THE RETURN OF THE KING

NEBUCHADNEZZAR, king of the mighty Babylonian empire, lay in his bed. His bed and its furnishings were as luxurious and comfortable as befitted the wealthiest and most powerful man in the world. But as far as Nebuchadnezzar's sleep was concerned, he might as well have been lying on a bed of nails. No matter how he twisted or turned, 'his sleep brake from him' (Dan. 2:1), and try though he might, he could get no rest. Sleepless nights were hardly unknown in Nebuchadnezzar's experience. The care of administering the massive empire was enough to see to that. But on this occasion, it was not the planning of fresh conquests, the faltering fortunes of a military campaign, or the intricate webs of court intrigue that robbed Nebuchadnezzar of his repose. On this occasion, it was a strange and troubling dream that kept Nebuchadnezzar from sleeping.

In his dream, Nebuchadnezzar had seen a great image of 'excellent brightness' and a 'terrible form' (Dan. 2:31). 'This image's head was of fine gold, his breast and his arms of silver, his belly and his thighs of brass, his legs of iron, his feet part of iron and part of clay' (vv. 32–33). It must have been an arresting sight. As Nebuchadnezzar beheld it in his dream, he must have wondered at the intricacy of its design. The form of this image, and every lineament of its surface spoke eloquently of human endeavour and achievement. And yet, even in sleep, the king must surely have noted with unease the insubstantial and insecure footing on which the whole image stood: a brittle basis of iron and pottery, immiscible and uncombined.

The king's vague feelings of unease were soon alarmingly exacerbated. The fragility of the image was about to be fully exposed. And it was not the passage of time, or the attrition of the elements, that would bring about the collapse of this vast structure. Rather the king saw:

> a stone was cut out without hands, which smote the image upon his feet that were of iron and clay, and brake them to pieces. Then was the iron, the clay, the brass, the silver, and the gold, broken to pieces together, and became like the chaff of the summer threshing floors; and the wind carried them away, that no place was found for them (vv. 34–35).

In contrast to the image, with its unmistakable signs of human design and execution, this stone was utterly apart from any human intervention. Apparently of no great moment, it nonetheless had the power to bring all the works of man into devastation and dust. Faced with such a scene, it is no wonder that Nebuchadnezzar's sleep broke from him.

Nebuchadnezzar sought in vain amongst the wise men of Babylon for an interpretation of his dream. After all of their wisdom proved unequal to the task, Daniel stepped forward to tell the dream and its interpretation. He explained that the image offered a summary of world history, the different and deteriorating metals representing the successive empires that would hold the dominion of the globe in their hands. Then, he explained the significance of 'the stone cut out without hands':

> And in the days of these kings shall the God of heaven set up a kingdom, which shall never be destroyed: and the kingdom shall not be left to other people, but it shall break in pieces and consume all these kingdoms, and it shall stand for ever (2:44).

The day would come when the long history of human rule would be brought to a crushing and crashing end.

In the previous chapter we considered some of the military manoeuvres that will take place as the hand of God arranges the nations for His purpose. We learned that an attack on the land of Israel by the united forces of the northern and southern powers will be utterly routed by Divine intervention. The western power, led by the beast, will respond ferociously to the aggression from the north and the south, and his armies will invade Israel, before cutting a conquering swath southwards. His progress will be halted by news of a massive invading army from the east, and he will 'go forth with great fury to destroy, and utterly to make away many' (Dan. 11:44). Thus will the words of God be fulfilled: 'I will gather all nations against Jerusalem to battle' (Zech. 14:2).

These warring global superpowers will converge on Jerusalem. The storied city will lie in ruins, one half of its occupants led into captivity, while looting soldiers sit in the streets, carelessly dividing their spoil. Battle will be pitched at the plain of Megiddo, for this great conflict is Armageddon, the battle of Megiddo. Great armies will face each other, weapons loaded, ready to lock horns in a battle to the death, a climactic conflict for total global supremacy. But as the armies wait for the word of command, a celestial convulsion will signal the arrival of a new combatant:

> Immediately after the tribulation of those days shall the sun be darkened, and the moon shall not give her light, and the stars shall fall from heaven, and the powers of the heavens shall be shaken: and then shall appear the sign of the Son of man in heaven: and then shall all the tribes of the earth mourn, and they shall see the Son of man coming in the clouds of heaven with power and great glory (Mt. 24:29–30).

Men will stare aghast as they see heaven opened, and

> behold a white horse; and He that sat upon him was called Faithful and True, and in righteousness He doth judge and make war. His eyes were as a flame of fire, and on His head were many crowns; and He had a name written, that no man knew, but He Himself. And He was clothed with a vesture dipped in blood: and His name is called The Word of God. And the armies which were in heaven followed Him upon white horses, clothed in fine linen, white and clean. (Rev. 19:11–14)

Many artists have tried to capture something of the dramatic impact of this scene, in one medium or another. We can be sure, however, that none of these efforts have succeeded in imparting a fraction of the impact of this arrival, as the King of kings and Lord of lords leads His army forth, conquering, and to conquer. All of mankind's military might will stand utterly abashed in the face of such a force. And yet, there will be no surrender. Instead, 'the beast, and the kings of the earth, and their armies' will turn their artillery heavenward in one last futile effort to 'make war against

Him that sat on the horse, and against His army' (Rev. 19:19). But not a missile will be launched, not a shot fired. The beast and the false prophet will be 'cast alive into a lake of fire burning with brimstone' (v. 20). Their followers will be 'slain with the sword of Him that sat upon the horse, which sword proceeded out of His mouth' (v. 21).

The conquering Christ will return in glorious triumph to the very point from which He left earth for heaven:

> And His feet shall stand in that day upon the mount of Olives, which is before Jerusalem on the east, and the mount of Olives shall cleave in the midst thereof toward the east and toward the west, and there shall be a very great valley; and half of the mountain shall remove toward the north, and half of it toward the south (Zech. 14:4).

Then He will return to the city of the great King. Battered by the armies of the centuries, this venerable city has seen many remarkable days. But nothing that she has seen will compare with this day. As Christ draws near, the glorious call and counter-call of Psalm 24 will ring out amongst the Judaean rocks:

> Lift up your heads, O ye gates;
>   And be ye lift up ye everlasting doors;
> And the King of glory shall come in.
>
>   Who is this King of glory?
> The LORD strong and mighty,
>   The LORD mighty in battle.
>
>
> Lift up your heads, O ye gates;

Even lift them up, ye everlasting doors;
And the King of glory shall come in.

Who is this King of glory?
The LORD of hosts, He is the King of glory! (vv.7–10)

CHAPTER FOURTEEN

THE GLORIOUS APPEARING

THE HISTORY OF THE WORLD is a complex tapestry of events, individuals, and ideas. Civilizations have risen and fallen. They have clashed in war, and cooperated in peace, they have built, and destroyed, and built again. The scale is so vast, and the action so complicated that we could easily forget that history has meaning, and that this meaning comes not from the deeds of man but from the decrees of God.

As the writer to the Hebrews demonstrates, history does have a plan, a pattern, and a purpose:

> Now once in the end of the world hath He appeared, to put away sin by the sacrifice of Himself. And as it is appointed unto men once to die, but after this the judgement: So Christ was once offered to bear the sins of many; and unto them that look for Him shall He appear the second time without sin unto salvation. (Heb. 9:26–28).

All of human history is summarised in these few verses. The ages past were preparatory, building towards the first advent of Christ, at 'the consummation of the ages' (JND). Now we look back to that unique event, but we also look forward to the second advent of Christ, as He appears the second time, apart from sin, unto salvation.

The first and second comings of Christ are the great poles of history, the two events that give meaning to the seemingly chaotic succession of people and events.

We are inclined – almost conditioned – to think of the Rapture when we think of the second coming of Christ. This is not surprising, for this is an imminent hope that is intimately ours, and we do long to meet our Lord in the air. But though the Rapture is a great event, it is only the first stage of the second coming of Christ. At the end of the Tribulation, He will be manifest in His public and glorious return to the earth, as sudden and shattering as a lightning bolt (Mt. 24:27). This event is one of the great prospects of Scripture, and it is, says Paul, our 'blessed hope' (Tit. 2:13). The return of Christ will be a dramatic and cataclysmic intervention in human history. It will have deep significance for the nations, for Israel, for Christ – and for us.

For the nations of the world, it will be a time of judgement. Revelation 19 describes Christ, seated on a white horse, coming as King of kings and Lord of lords, destroying utterly the armies who have gathered together to make war against the Lamb. But the blasting of man's rebellion, and the banishment of its leaders will only be the beginning of the judgement of the nations. After the manifestation of Christ, and His victory over the armies of men, the event generally – though perhaps unhelpfully, as it will be individuals who are judged – known as the judgement of the living nations will take place:

> When the Son of man shall come in His glory, and all the holy angels with Him, then shall He sit upon the throne of His glory: And before Him shall be gathered all nations: and He shall separate them one from another, as a shepherd divideth his sheep from the goats. ... Then shall the King say unto

them on His right hand, Come, ye blessed of My
Father, inherit the kingdom prepared for you from
the foundation of the world: For I was a hungred,
and ye gave Me meat: I was thirsty, and ye gave Me
drink: I was a stranger, and ye took Me in: Naked,
and ye clothed Me: I was sick, and ye visited Me: I
was in prison, and ye came unto Me. (Mt. 25:31–36,
see also Joel 3:11–12).

From John 3:3, Matthew 18:3, and a number of other passages we know that those who enter the kingdom must be born again. These sheep are those who have heard and responded to the gospel of the kingdom, which has been preached during the Tribulation by the 144,000 witnesses (Rev. 7). The way in which these people have treated God's messengers is an index to their response to the message. This was true when Rahab sheltered the spies (Josh. 2, Heb. 11:31), and when the Lord sent out seventy witnesses (Lk. 10:3–16), and it will certainly be the case during the Tribulation, when harbouring one of the persecuted Jewish remnant could have appalling consequences. Only those who are born again will dare to express fellowship with these persecuted believers, and having been born again, they are the blessed of the Father, and will enter into the enjoyment of the earthly millennial kingdom.

For Israel, Christ's return will be a time of restoration. God still has a place for His earthly people and, when Christ returns, a faithful remnant will hail their Messiah. In a world where supersessionism (the belief that the Church has replaced Israel in the purpose of God) runs rife, we do well to remember that Paul's great statement that 'the gifts and calling of God are without repentance' (Rom. 11.29), is made in the context of his discussion of God's faithfulness to Israel. If we rob Israel of their hope, we deny the character and faithfulness of

God, and rob the Church of her confidence in Him. Israel has failed God many times and in many ways but God has never failed Israel, and when the Lord Jesus is manifest 'they shall look upon [Him] Whom they have pierced, and they shall mourn for Him, as one mourneth for his only son, and shall be in bitterness for Him, as one that is in bitterness for his firstborn' (Zech.12.10). There will be judgement for Israel. This is depicted in the parables of Matthew 25, and described in Ezekiel 20:34–38 and Malachi 3:2–5. Those who have trusted Christ and acknowledged His claims will enter into millennial blessing. Those who have made no preparation will be cast into outer darkness. Ultimately, the nation will be restored to relationship with God:

> I will bring the third part through the fire, and will refine them as silver is refined, and will try them as gold is tried: they shall call on My name, and I will hear them: I will say, It is My people: and they shall say, The LORD is my God (Zech.13:9).

For Christ it will be a time of vindication. The world last saw Jesus of Nazareth on a cross. To the Jew it was a symbol of one accursed; to the Gentile it indicated a felon so base, so contemptible as to merit only the agonizing and shameful death of a rebellious slave. Though the apostles preached the resurrection and ascension of Christ, for many that verdict has never been reversed: our Lord is still despised. But here, on earth, where He was rejected, and amongst those who rejected Him, Christ will be vindicated. God will have the last word as to the true character of His Son. God's time is set when He will show His Son as 'the blessed and only Potentate, the King of kings, and Lord of lords' (1 Tim. 6:15). Christ humbled Himself; God will exalt Him and 'at the name of Jesus every knee should bow ... and

… every tongue … confess that Jesus Christ is Lord, to the glory of God the Father' (Phil. 2:10–11).

The manifestation of Christ is our 'blessed hope'. To see our Saviour given His rightful place, to see Israel restored, and to see the unrighteousness of the world judged and set right will gladden our hearts and answer our prayers. However, God has something beyond observation in mind for the Church. We will not be distant observers of Christ's manifestation; we will be involved in it as participants. Christ is not coming back alone, we will accompany Him 'upon white horses, clothed in fine linen, white and clean' (Rev. 19:14). What grace it is that allows us not only to witness but to share His glory and His triumph.

Like every hope of the believer, this anticipation reaches into our present experience. Paul points the persecuted Thessalonian believers to the day 'when the Lord Jesus shall be revealed from heaven with His mighty angels' (2 Thess. 1:7), when their suffering will be recompensed. It is in the light of their part in this glorious event that he prays:

> that our God would count you worthy of this calling, and fulfil all the good pleasure of His goodness, and the work of faith with power: That the name of our Lord Jesus Christ may be glorified in you, and ye in Him, according to the grace of our God and the Lord Jesus Christ (vv. 11–12).

What the apostle prayed for these believers in the light of the manifestation of Christ ought surely to be our prayer as we anticipate that tremendous day.

Chapter Fifteen

The Certainty of the Millennium

IN AN EARLIER CHAPTER in this book, we considered the dream of King Nebuchadnezzar. We saw the great prophetic significance of the seemingly insignificant stone 'cut off without hands', that struck the feet of the great image, bringing all that spoke of human ingenuity, design, and execution to ignominious dust, blown away by the wind. Our consideration stopped there, but Nebuchadnezzar's dream and Daniel's interpretation did not, for history does not end, and God's purposes are not complete when Christ is manifest in glory and His enemies are reduced to nothing before Him. In his dream, the wondering king watched as 'the stone that smote the image became a great mountain, and filled the whole earth' (Dan. 2:35), and Daniel concisely explained the significance of what he had seen:

> And in the days of these kings shall the God of heaven set up a kingdom, which shall never be destroyed: and the kingdom shall not be left to other people, but it shall break in pieces and consume all these kingdoms, and it shall stand for ever (Dan. 2:44).

The devastating destruction of the kings and the kingdoms of earth is only a prelude to the establishment of the kingdom of the Lord Jesus Christ. Each of the metals that composed the image represented an historical earthly kingdom, and the stone that replaces them must also represent an actual earthly kingdom.

King Nebuchadnezzar saw this event from an earthly point of view. Towards the end of the Revelation, John is granted a heavenly perspective:

> And I saw an angel come down from heaven ... And he laid hold on the dragon, that old serpent, which is the Devil, and Satan, and bound him a thousand years, And cast him into the bottomless pit, and shut him up, and set a seal upon him, that he should deceive the nations no more, till the thousand years should be fulfilled: and after that he must be loosed a little season. And I saw thrones, and they sat upon them, and judgement was given unto them... and they lived and reigned with Christ a thousand years (Rev. 20:1-4).

Not only will the kingdoms of men be swept away, Satan himself will be bound, his baleful influence eliminated from the world as Christ and His redeemed reign for a thousand years – the glorious period that we call the Millennium.

There are, perhaps, few scriptural truths that have been so distorted or denied as the millennial reign of Christ. Though believers in the centuries following the death of Christ held the doctrine, others, swayed by the influence of Greek philosophy and Gnostic teaching, denied it. Origen (AD 185-254) developed an allegorical way of reading Scripture, which was dismissive of the literal sense, and sought a deeper, spiritual meaning behind the text of Scripture. This laid the basis for the teaching of Augustine (AD 354–430). Augustine's philosophical and political views, coupled with an allegorical approach to Scripture, led him to deny the truth of the reign of Christ on earth. Instead, he argued that Satan had been bound at Calvary, and that the Church – by which Augustine meant the Roman church – was already reigning spiritually. Augustine is the father of amillennialism, and his views formed the basis for the eschatological teaching of the Roman Catholic Church and, later, of the Reformers.

For most of the past two thousand years, the truth of the Millennium has been denied and denigrated by those who were unwilling – for whatever reason – to take God at His word. But all their denials should not cause us to doubt that Christ 'shall have dominion also from sea to sea' (Ps. 72:8). There are many reasons why this is so: we will consider two of them in the remainder of this chapter.

GOD'S WORD DECLARES IT

This, all by itself, should be a sufficient reason to believe in the truth of the Millennium. It is clearly and unambiguously presented in the Word of God. It is true that only Revelation 20 gives the duration of Christ's reign – though it does give it six times in as many verses. However, Old Testament prophecy is saturated with details about that reign, about the religious, social, and ecological conditions that will mark it. Amillennialists will point out that Revelation is a book filled with symbolism. That is true, but it is also the case that Revelation is very precise about time – about years, months, and days. It is difficult, without significant special pleading, to deny that this passage clearly presents the literal reign of Christ for one thousand years, and the associated reign of all those who have a part in the first resurrection. We have already seen that

God fulfils prophecy literally. We would never think of spiritualizing the many and detailed prophecies concerning the first coming of Christ, nor should we contemplate treating the prophecies of His second coming in this way.

GOD'S CHARACTER DEMANDS IT

The writer to the Hebrews reminds us that it is 'impossible for God to lie' (6:18). This great truth is of incalculable value to us. All of the exceeding great and precious promises that God has made to us are underwritten by the immutable truth of His character. But even as we cherish the application of this truth to ourselves, we ought carefully to notice the context in which it appears. The writer reminds us of the 'immutability of [God's] counsel' expressed in His covenant promise to Abraham, and confirmed with the covenant oath. In His sovereign grace, God chose to bind Himself to Abraham, and his descendants in a solemn, unbreakable, and unconditional commitment.

In a similar way the truth that 'the gifts and calling of God are without repentance' (Rom. 11:29) encourages the heart of every believer, giving us the confidence that God is no fickle despot, ruled by whim, but is faithful and dependable. Again, though, this great statement is made in the context of God's covenant dealings with Israel. God's refusal to renounce His failing earthly people is the example and evidence of the faithfulness of His character.

It is vital that we do not miss the significance of this. God has made unilateral and unconditional promises to Abraham and his descendants. Nothing could be more sure than God's promise, but in grace He confirmed it with an oath, in order that Abraham and Israel could have no doubt about the certainty that God would perform His promise. Those promises have never yet had their complete fulfilment and, if there is no Millennium, they never will be fulfilled.

God's covenant with David, too, is unconditional and immutable, and Scripture states its certainty in the strongest terms:

> Thus saith the LORD, If ye can break My covenant of the day, and My covenant of the night, and that there should not be day and night in their season; Then may also My covenant be broken with David My servant, that he should not have a son to reign upon his throne (Jer. 33:20–21).

It is, then, entirely in concord with Scripture to say that the earthly reign of Christ (for David's is unquestionably an earthly throne) is as sure as the rising of the sun tomorrow morning.

To deny the Millennium, then, is to make a liar of God, and a fiction of His Word. Nor is the situation much improved by those amillennialists who argue that the promises made to Israel are being fulfilled in a spiritual way to the Church. It would be interesting to know how such an individual would react if his employer, who had entered into a binding contract to pay a certain salary every month, were to tell him that his pay cheque was a spiritual, rather than a literal, one. In such circumstances, none of us would dream of suggesting that the employer had kept his word. We would excoriate him as a juggler with words at best, and an unscrupulous liar at worst. God made literal promises to Abraham and to his seed. To suggest that God subsequently 'moved the goal posts', redefining what the promises meant, or to whom they were made, is a grave insult to His character.

Beyond this, the denial of a Millennium in which the promises to Israel will be fulfilled grievously undermines the believer's confidence in God. As demonstrated by the passages mentioned, the faithfulness of God to Israel is a source of wonder and reassurance, and an invaluable insight into the character of the God that we have come to know. Therefore, while it is true that a denial of God's future purpose for Israel robs that nation of its special place, that is only a beginning: it also impoverishes the Church and, most seriously of all, touches the glory and greatness of God.

The truth that God cannot lie was, to the suffering Hebrew believers, a 'strong consolation'. May we, too, rejoice in the steadfastness of our God, and, eschewing hermeneutical gymnastics and interpretative gyrations, be prepared to take God at His word. And doing so, let us look forward to the glorious revelation and reign of the rejected Saviour, Who 'must reign, till He hath put all enemies under His feet' (1 Cor. 15:25).

CHAPTER SIXTEEN

THE CHARACTER OF THE MILLENNIUM

WE HAVE ALREADY SEEN that the term 'Millennium' does not appear in Scripture. While the word may not occur, the truth of the earthly reign of Christ is found throughout the Bible, and the term is an accurate one to describe a reign that extends for one thousand years. There are, however, a number of other terms used in Scripture to speak of the reign of Christ. Each one unfolds particular truth about the character and consequences of that reign, and merits our careful consideration.

THE REGENERATION

'Then answered Peter and said unto him, Behold, we have forsaken all, and followed Thee; what shall we have therefore? And Jesus said unto them, Verily I say unto you, That ye which have followed Me, in the regeneration when the Son of man shall sit in the throne of His glory, ye also shall sit upon twelve thrones, judging the twelve tribes of Israel' (Mt. 19:27–28).

The course of world history is anything but smooth. Morally, ideologically, financially, and militarily, it is marked by revolution and counter-revolution, by decline and revival, by meteoric rises and precipitous falls. But often, the more things change, the more they stay the same. Even the most dramatic and far-reaching revolution does little to change the overall course of life on earth. Not so the establishment of Christ's kingdom. The Lord Jesus describes it as 'the regeneration', or rebirth. The word is used in only one other place in Scripture (Tit. 3:5), where it refers to the new birth of the believer. The Millennium will not be a revival – it will be a rebirth. The planet will be born again, and the change will be as dramatic – and fundamental – as that which salvation brings to the life of an individual.

TIMES OF REFRESHING AND RESTITUTION

'Repent ye therefore, and be converted, that your sins may be blotted out, when the times of refreshing shall come from the presence of the Lord. And He shall send Jesus Christ, which before was preached unto you: Whom the heaven must receive until the times of restitution of all things, which God hath spoken by the mouth of all His holy prophets since the world began' (Acts 3:19–22).

In this great address to the men of Israel, the apostle Peter used two beautiful expressions – both found only here in Scripture – to describe the effects of Christ's return to earth from heaven, and His ensuing reign.

'Refreshing' is literally 'a cooling' (the Latin Vulgate translates the word with the familiar-looking *'refrigerium'*). The idea of a refreshing and restoring coolness in a hot and arid climate eloquently conveys what the Millennium will mean for this parched and weary earth. Worn out by injustice and oppression, battered by violence and inhumanity, she is sorely in need of the refreshment of the Messiah's manifestation, when, from the presence of God, through 'the windows of heaven' (Mal. 3:10) will flow a restoring and revitalising stream. In the language of Psalm 72, 'He shall come down like rain upon the mown grass: as showers that water the earth' (v. 6). His righteous reign will bring refreshment, as 'judgment [will] run down as waters, and righteousness as a mighty stream' (Amos 5:24).

The Millennium will also be a time of restoration. This is the dominant idea in the phrase 'the times of restitution of all things'. Notice the comprehensiveness of Peter's statement – 'all things' will be restored in that day. So much was lost in the Fall. Humanity was debased and depraved, and with it all of creation was 'made subject to vanity' and brought into 'the bondage of corruption' (Rom. 8:20–21). In this bondage, it groans and travails in pain to the present day. Adam's disobedience caused far-reaching devastation. But at Calvary, the Saviour 'restored that which [He] took not away' (Ps. 69:4). The restoration accomplished by His work at the cross has yet to be fully realised, but, as the Redeemer is revealed, and we are manifest with Him, the creation will be delivered from bondage, and 'into the glorious liberty of the children of God' (Rom. 8:21).

But the Holy Spirit, through Peter, extends the scope of 'all things' beyond the restoration of a fallen creation. A few verses later, Peter alludes to the Abrahamic covenant, and its millennial fulfilment:

> Ye are the children of ... the covenant which God made with our fathers, saying unto Abraham, And in thy seed shall all the kindreds of the earth be blessed (Acts 3:25).

At the time when Peter spoke, Israel had fallen to a low point, but a few decades later, she would fall even further. She had been deprived of her theocracy, and would shortly lose her Temple. All that she had pointed to with pride, all that spoke of her unique status amongst the nations, would be stripped from her, and her people would be scattered to the four winds. They would learn the bitter reality of the burden they had so lightly assumed when they cried 'His blood be on us and on our children' (Mt. 27:25). But the great wonder of God's programme for the nation is that, in spite of their failure and rebellion, in spite of their rejection of the Messiah, they have not 'stumbled that they should fall' (Rom. 11:11) Rather, 'blindness in part is happened to Israel, until the fulness of the Gentiles be come in. And so all Israel shall be saved' (Rom. 11:25–26). We cannot allow the pernicious doctrines of Replacement Theology to erode our appreciation of the faithfulness of God. The Church has neither replaced nor displaced Israel, and the time will come when all will be restored, and she will be 'the head, and not the tail' (Deut. 28:13).

This time of restoration was long promised – 'since the world began'. It is exceedingly precious to know that the first prophecy of restoration and of a ruler – the proto-evangelical promise of the Seed of the woman, Who would bruise the serpent's head (Gen 3:15) – is made even before God pronounces His curse on humanity and on creation. And from that point onwards, Scripture re-echoes with glorious words of promise, affirming and reaffirming that there will be a time of restoration when all that is wrong will be put right, and all that has been lost will be recovered.

THE DISPENSATION OF THE FULNESS OF TIMES

'That in the dispensation of the fulness of times He might gather together in one all things in Christ, both which are in heaven, and which are on earth; even in Him: In Whom also we have obtained an inheritance' (Eph. 1:10–11).

The first advent of the Lord Jesus was the climax of history, taking place at 'the consummation of the ages'

(Heb. 9:26, JND). We, in this dispensation of grace, are those 'on whom the ends of the ages have come' (1 Cor. 10:11, NET). But though this dispensation is the climax of history, it is not its completion. God's purpose for the nations, for Israel, for the Church, and for His Son awaits its full accomplishment at the 'fulness of times'. The word 'fulness' conveys the idea of order and completion. It is the word used for a ship, when the full complement of its crew is on board, with every man at his station. It beautifully conveys the conditions that will exist in the millennial kingdom, when God's purpose will be seen in full operation, and when the nations, Israel, and the Church will occupy their rightful place, and fulfil their ordained function. And over it all, heading up all things, will be the Lord Jesus Christ, at last acknowledged and obeyed by all. There will be great blessing for those who participate in millennial glory. But the greatest glory will be the vindication and glorification of the 'once despised Jesus' on the earth where He was rejected.

These scriptures outline for us the character of the coming kingdom. Rebirth, refreshment, restoration, and completeness will all mark those thousand triumphant years of vindication and victory when 'He shall bear the glory, and shall sit and rule upon his throne' (Zech. 6:13)

CHAPTER SEVENTEEN

THE CITIZENS AND CONDITIONS OF THE MILLENNIUM

IN WHAT IS arguably Shakespeare's greatest play, Hamlet, having just learned of his father's murder, and the rottenness that lies at the heart of the state of Denmark, laments that 'the times are out of joint'. The phrase expresses his consciousness that something has gone badly and fundamentally wrong with the world. There can hardly be anyone who has not, at one time or another, shared Hamlet's feelings. We cannot scan the headlines without appreciating that the world is not as it should be. Man's inhumanity to man, his failure in the stewardship of creation, and the vicious violence that marks a nature red in tooth and claw all blazon the truth that we live in a disjointed world. Humanity's awareness of this has led many men and women to attempt to imagine and inaugurate their own millennial Utopias. Their efforts have always met with failure, and, not infrequently, with disaster. Man's fallen mind cannot devise, nor his sinful character implement, a perfect world. But a perfect world will be inaugurated, designed by Divine wisdom, enforced by Divine authority, and enabled by Divine power.

THE CITIZENS OF THE MILLENNIUM

The millennial kingdom will be unique in history in that it will include among its citizens those who have died and been resurrected. Revelation 20:6 tells us that all who have had a part in the first resurrection will live and reign with Christ. This first resurrection will take place in a number of stages. Christ's resurrection provided the prototype, and He, as firstfruits, will be followed by the saints of this dispensation, at the Rapture, and subsequently by the Old Testament saints, and by those who have been martyred during the Tribulation. At the commencement of the Millennium the first resurrection will be complete, and all who, throughout the ages, have been justified by faith will live and reign with Christ.

The kingdom will also include those who have never died. After the manifestation of Christ, the judgement of the living nations will take place. There the sheep will be separated from the goats. The sheep, those latter-day Rahabs who, by their refusal to take the mark of the beast and their refreshment of God's persecuted remnant, will have given evidence of their faith in Christ, will 'inherit the kingdom prepared for [them] from the foundation of the world' (Mt. 25:34). Resurrected saints and those who have never died will join together in their enjoyment of the presence of Christ, just as they did so long ago in the home in Bethany (Jn 12).

Thus, all who enter into the millennial kingdom will be believers. During the thousand years, however, human generation will continue – 'the streets of the city shall be full of boys and girls playing' (Zech. 8:5). Those who are born will possess the same fallen nature as you and I, and they will need to be saved. No doubt many will, but, notwithstanding the visible and immanent evidences of the greatness and goodness of God and the perfections of Christ's reign, there will be many who will not believe. Disobedience to Divine law will bring immediate punishment, and so they will feign obedience, but ultimately these unbelievers will furnish ample evidence that they never possessed Divine life.

THE CONDITIONS OF THE MILLENNIUM

Two vitally important conditions will mark the Millennium. Christ will reign, and Satan will be bound. The administration of Christ, and the absence of the tempter will utterly transform life on earth. Beyond this, Scripture provides an enormous amount of detail about the conditions that will mark the Millennium. Even a cursory survey would require more space than we have, but we will highlight some of the most significant conditions that will mark the reign of Christ.

Ecologically, the Millennium will be marked by the reversal of the effects of Adam's fall. Creation will be 'delivered from the bondage of corruption into the glorious liberty of the children of God' (Rom. 8:21). Christ's return to earth will be attended by seismic transformation (Zech. 14), and the parched deserts of the world will be transformed:

> The wilderness and the solitary place shall be glad for them; and the desert shall rejoice, and blossom as the rose. It shall blossom abundantly (Isa. 35:1–2).

> In the wilderness shall waters break out, and streams in the desert. And the parched ground shall become a pool, and the thirsty land springs of water (Isa. 35:6–7).

Food shortage will be a forgotten concern as earth will be marked by fruitfulness never seen since Eden: 'There shall be an handful of corn in the earth upon the top of the mountains; the fruit thereof shall shake like Lebanon' (Ps. 72:16).

Prosperity will go hand-in-hand with peace. The violence and death that join every link in the food chain will be halted, and predator and prey will co-exist in perfect harmony:

> The wolf also shall dwell with the lamb, and the leopard shall lie down with the kid ... and a little child shall lead them. ... The lion shall eat straw like the ox. ... They shall not hurt nor destroy in all My holy mountain (Isa. 11:6–9).

Governmentally, too, the reign will be marked by peace. For the first time in history, the nations will be ruled by One Who has both the power and the authority to reign and His reign will be one of justice and equity – and of unchallenged authority:

> He shall have dominion also from sea to sea, and from the river unto the ends of the earth. ... All kings shall fall down before Him: all nations shall serve Him' (Ps. 72:8–11).

> And He shall judge among the nations, and shall rebuke many people: and they shall beat their swords into plowshares, and their spears into pruninghooks: nation shall not lift up sword against nation, neither shall they learn war any more (Isa. 2:4).

In contrast to the governments of men, His policies will not be swayed by lobbyists or pressure groups. Rather, 'He shall judge the poor of the people, He shall save the children of the needy, and shall break in pieces the oppressor' (Ps. 72:4).

Spiritually, the Millennium will see the restoration of some of the service of the Temple. Ezekiel 40–48 outline the details of the service that will be carried on when the glory of God, once again, fills the house:

> And, behold, the glory of the God of Israel came from the way of the east: and His voice was like a noise of many waters: and the earth shined with His glory. ... Behold, the glory of the LORD filled the house (Ezek. 43:2,5).

Animal sacrifices will be offered once again on the altars, not now for the putting away of sin, but for cleansing from ritual defilement. The Temple will no longer be open to the Jews alone. Now it will be the global centre of worship, and annual attendance at the feast of tabernacles will be mandatory for all peoples (Zech. 14:16–19). For the first time in her history, Israel will perform the purpose that God intended, to be a kingdom of priests.

The processes of secularization have inexorably squeezed religion out of our world, banishing it from public life and forcing it to the margins in every way possible. In the Millennium, the worship of God will permeate every aspect of life, and the secular will become sacred: 'In that day shall there be upon the bells of the horses, HOLINESS UNTO THE LORD... Yea, every pot in Jerusalem and in Judah shall be holiness unto the LORD of hosts' (Zech. 14:20–21). The darkness of ignorance, and the delusion of error will be banished from every corner of creation, 'for the earth shall be filled with the knowledge of the glory of the LORD, as the waters cover the sea' (Hab. 2:14)

Chapter Eighteen

THE CONCLUSION OF THE MILLENNIUM

ONE OF THE MOST IMPRESSIVE FEATURES of Biblical prophecy must surely be its certainty. While human forecasts and projections abound in ifs, buts, and maybes, the face-saving language of conditionality, God's prophecies are couched in terms of steadfast certainty. Again and again we read the word 'must', communicating not just probability, but necessity and obligation.

Scripture speaks of many 'musts' in relation to the first coming of Christ. The 'must' of His betrayal (Acts 1:16), of His rejection, suffering, death, and resurrection (Mt. 16:21; Mk 8:31, Lk. 9:22; 24:7; Acts 17:3); of His 'lifting up' at Calvary (Jn 3:14; 12:34); and of His exaltation to the Father's right hand (Acts 3:21) all remind us that there was nothing haphazard about the life of the Lord Jesus. He moved conscious of the 'must' that Scripture be accomplished (Lk. 22:37; 24:44), and the hand of God arranged men and events so that not a single detail was found in default.

There are many 'musts' in relation to the second coming of the Lord Jesus. There is the 'must' of the

Tribulation (Mt. 24:6; Mk 13:7; Lk. 21:9). For the believer, there is the 'must' of the resurrection and the transformation of our mortal bodies (1 Cor. 15:53), and of the judgement seat of Christ (2 Cor. 5:10). Gloriously, there is the 'must' of Christ's reign (1 Cor. 15:25). Revelation does not describe the things which could or which might be, but the things which 'must ... come to pass' (Rev. 1:1), 'which must be hereafter' (Rev. 4:1), 'the things which must shortly be done' (Rev. 22:6). History cannot defy Divine direction: God's purpose is inexorable and His plan inevitable.

With the establishment of the millennial kingdom, almost all of the 'musts' of prophecy will have been implemented. Believers will have been raised and glorified, their service assessed and rewarded. The turmoil of the Tribulation will have passed, and Christ will be reigning in righteousness. But one more 'must' remains. We have already seen how, at the beginning of the Millennium, an angel will bind Satan and:

> cast him into the bottomless pit, and shut him up, and set a seal upon him, that he should deceive the nations no more, till the thousand years should be fulfilled: and after that he must be loosed a little season (Rev. 20:3).

Satan will be bound, but he must be loosed.

The necessity of this event may well seem difficult to understand. Humanity will have enjoyed a thousand year period of peace and prosperity unparalleled by any other. And this blessing will be possible because Satan is bound: his baneful influence and corrupting blandishments removed from the world. His confinement will not have improved his character, or transformed his intentions. Released, he will exert himself to bring an end to the order that has been imposed on earth, and to the happiness of its citizens. Again he 'shall go out to deceive the nations which are in the four quarters of the earth, Gog and Magog, to gather them together to battle' (Rev. 20:8), fomenting a final and futile rebellion against God and His Christ. History, during the Millennium, had seemed likely to end on a wave of blessing; now, inevitably, it will come to a close with a torrent of judgement.

Why is it essential that Satan be released? The history of God's dealings with mankind does provide us with one answer, at least, to this question. The Bible does not present history as a homogeneous whole. Rather, we learn that God has divided time into a series of periods called 'ages' (often translated as 'world', e.g. 1 Cor. 10:11; Eph. 2:7; Col. 1:26; Heb. 1:2; 9:26) or 'generations' (Acts 14:15–16 [translated 'times']; Eph. 3:4–5; Col. 1:26). These periods are each marked by a particular 'dispensation' or form of administration (1 Cor. 9:17; Eph. 1:10–12; 3:2–7; Col. 1:25–26), and we frequently speak of them as 'the dispensations'. Each dispensation is marked by a new revelation from God, and a new responsibility that derives from that revelation. Throughout history, from Eden onwards, God has repeatedly tested mankind. The Millennium, the seventh and final dispensation, is no exception.

It is important to understand the way in which God tests mankind. Sometimes we test things to determine their character. We wait in apprehension for the results of school examinations or medical tests because we do not know what the result will be – we are testing to determine. But we also test to demonstrate character. Imagine an engineer whose design is being tested. We would not expect to find him perspiring and pacing the floor. He knows what his design can withstand: the testing is not to determine its character, but to demonstrate it. Thus it is with Divine testing. God is never surprised by the results of His tests. Rather, He tests humanity to demonstrate, again and again, the failure of unregenerate man to worship and obey God.

Humanity's first failure set the pattern for all that would follow. The deception of the serpent, the feeling that God was a domineering tyrant Who did not have humanity's best interests at heart, and the wilful choice to disobey the Word of God have been repeated down through the centuries. And as mankind has repeated its failure, it has also repeatedly sought to excuse it. In Eden, Adam and Eve both sought to pass the blame – Adam to Eve, and Eve to the serpent – and their descendants have continually sought to locate the blame somewhere – anywhere – other than where it really lies – the heart of man.

In our day, men and women continue to deny that the heart of the problem is the problem of the heart. As they seek to account for the ills of society, sociologists and psychologists insist that we are not depraved, but deprived, that the problems of mankind are the product of failed nurturing rather than of a fallen nature. Individuals will excuse their failure to believe by complaining that God has never shown Himself, that the evidence of His existence is insufficient to compel their belief.

The release of Satan will demonstrate that these excuses are mere empty pretence. For one thousand years, men and women will have enjoyed a perfect environment, a fruitful creation, a well-ordered society, and the perfect rule of the King of kings. 'The earth shall be filled with the knowledge of the glory of the LORD' (Hab. 2:14) and His existence and goodness alike will be undeniably manifest. But even in these surroundings, and with these blessings, unregenerate man will fail.

It is important to remember that there will be unregenerate individuals on earth during the Millennium. As we have seen, only those who are saved will enter the kingdom. However, the children born during the period will still be born with a sinful nature and will need to trust Christ for themselves. Punishment for sin will be immediate (Jer. 31:30) and severe (Isa. 65:20). Because of this, God's 'enemies will give feigned obedience' (Ps. 66:3, NASB) to Him. These individuals will be Satan's willing dupes. They will gather behind him for one last rebellion, one final effort to 'break [God's] bands asunder' (Ps. 2:3). Their number will be 'as the sand of the sea' (Rev. 20:8). The focus of their fury is the city of Jerusalem, the seat of the Messiah's government: 'they went up on the breadth of the earth, and compassed the camp of the saints about, and the beloved city' (Rev. 20:9). The fury of their rebellion will be matched by its futility. As the last in a long series of sieges is set about Jerusalem:

> fire came down from God out of heaven, and devoured them. And the devil that deceived them was cast into the lake of fire and brimstone, where the beast and the false prophet are, and shall be tormented day and night for ever and ever (20:9–10).

Throughout history, humanity has been seduced time and again by the myth of human perfectibility and the chimera of historical progress. The 'must' of Satan's release will demonstrate beyond denial the fact that humanity's only hope is found in the unmerited, unearned, and undeserved grace of God.

Chapter Nineteen

THE GREAT WHITE THRONE

THE AREOPAGUS WAS AGOG. The cream of Athenian society, those insatiable seekers after intellectual innovation, had gathered together to hear some new thing. As they gazed on the diminutive figure waiting to address them, they felt sure that they were in for a treat: the exposition of a philosophical system that would be unfamiliar, stimulating even to their jaded academic palates. As the apostle stepped forward, the buzz of conversation died, and all Athens strained forward to hear what he had to say.

What they heard was one of the great apostolic discourses of Acts. On previous occasions when the apostle preached, he had been able to assume some level of acquaintance with Scripture, but this audience was deep in the darkness of pagan polytheism. As Paul spoke that darkness was pierced by a brilliant gleam of Divine revelation. Paul wasted no time in proclaiming the greatness of God. His listeners must have been thrilled as he introduced them to the Creator of the world, and the Giver of life. He spoke of a God Who is more than silver or gold or stone, Who transcends His own creation. And he presented a God Who desires a relationship with humanity, Who has made Himself known to His creature. The expectations of his audience had not been disappointed – this was a message very different from the usual arid speculation of the usual philosophers.

But Paul was still speaking, and as he did so a ripple of consternation ran through the crowd. This creating revealing God, Paul told them, had, in the past, overlooked their ignorance, but now He required – commanded – their repentance. Worse still, that repentance was required because a resurrected Man was going to judge the world. Small murmurs grew to louder altercations, and the crowd disintegrated into disagreement – some prevaricating, some mocking, and just a few believing.

The command to repent and the warning of judgement are never a popular or palatable part of the gospel. Yet, if we are to preach it faithfully we must follow Paul's example and warn sinners of a judgement that is universal – with implications for 'all men everywhere'; inevitable – the day is Divinely-appointed; and assured by the resurrection of the Lord Jesus.

The details of this judgement are provided in Revelation 20:11–15. John sees the court prepared – a 'great white throne' set up in space. The throne speaks of authority, and its greatness emphasises the cosmic jurisdiction and boundless authority of this court. The whiteness of the throne denotes the holiness of the Judge, His unquestionable moral authority. This presiding Judge is described as the One 'from Whose face the earth and the heaven fled away' (v. 11). Acts 17:31 and John 5:22 identify the One Who sits as Judge – He is the Man ordained, the Son of God, into Whose hand God has committed all judgement, Himself God (Rev. 20:12). So absolute is the holiness of this Judge that creation scurries to hide from His face.

John then describes the individuals present at this scene. He sees 'the dead, small and great, stand before God'. These are those spoken of in verse 5 as 'the rest of the dead'. These men and women, drawn from every imaginable demographic and social class, have never exercised faith in God, have never been justified or born again. Thus they had no part amongst the blessed of the first resurrection, and thus they now stand before God to receive their final judgement. 'Death and hell delivered up the dead which were in them' (v. 13), souls and bodies reunited to hear the pronouncement of their eternal doom.

As they stand, evidence is produced: 'the books were opened: and another book was opened, which is the book of life: and the dead were judged out of those things which were written in the books, according to their works' (v. 12). How solemn it is to think of these volumes, the record of the works of every individual who has lived, a minute and meticulous record of every thought, act, and word. Every action will be weighed. But they are weighed not to determine guilt, but to apportion punishment. Apart from the 'book of life', nothing that is written in these books can avert punishment. And, before sentence is delivered, the 'book of life' is opened, and its pages scanned. No one who stands before the great white throne will be found written in the book of life, but it is opened and examined as a last, incontrovertible proof of the sinner's guilt.

When that guilt has been demonstrated beyond challenge the sentence is passed: 'whosoever was not found written in the book of life was cast into the lake of fire' (v.15). 'This is the second death' (v. 14). How inexpressibly solemn it is to think of men and women, boys and girls, fathers and mothers, sons and daughters, being cast, with full consciousness, into 'everlasting fire, prepared for the devil and his angels' (Mt. 25:41), beginning an eternity of torment 'where their worm dieth not, and the fire is not quenched' (Mk. 9:44). As we survey the tragic terrifying scene, let us take a moment to consider whether our names are written in the Lamb's book of life, guaranteeing our eternal safety. In the light of the open pit, let us make sure that we have fled to Christ for refuge (Heb. 6:18). And let all of us who have the responsibility of preaching the gospel to perishing sinners lay to our hearts the example of the apostle, and faithfully warn our hearers of the inevitability of coming judgement.

When the judgement of the great white throne has been completed, the final act in the drama of time will take place. Creation, which has witnessed so much of the greatness and grace of God, and of the failure and fragility of man, will have fulfilled its purpose, and will be folded up like a worn-out garment (Heb. 1:10–12). Notwithstanding the speculations of scientists and the musings of poets, the universe will not simply wind down, the world will end not with a whimper, but a bang: 'the heavens shall pass away with a great noise, and the elements shall melt with fervent heat, the earth also and the works that are therein shall be burned up' (2 Pet. 3:10). Every trace and taint of sin will be finally and ferociously eradicated, and a new creation will be brought into being 'wherein dwelleth righteousness' (2 Pet. 3:13).

The telescope of Scripture allows us to see clear to the far horizon of time. But even as Peter describes the events that will mark the end of the old creation and the inauguration of the new he reminds us that prophetic truth is not intended for mere speculative contemplation, but to mark and mould our lives in the present:

Seeing then that all these things shall be dissolved, what manner of persons ought ye to be in all holy conversation and godliness, Looking for and hasting unto the coming of the day of God, wherein the heavens being on fire shall be dissolved, and the elements shall melt with fervent heat? (2 Pet. 3:11–12).

Chapter Twenty

The Eternal State

OUR STUDY OF BIBLE PROPHECY has taken us to the far shore of time, to the horizon of history. Only Scripture gives us this sort of perspective, allowing us to see from the creation of time 'in the beginning' (Gen. 1:1) right through to its conclusion. But it also allows us to see beyond time, to the dawn of eternity, and into 'the day of eternity' (2 Pet. 3:18, JND).

It is a remarkable thing that God allows us to take the telescope of Scripture and peer into eternity. It is even more remarkable that we display such a reluctance to do so. When planning a trip we usually spend time thinking about our destination, consulting travel guides and visitor reviews, planning where we will go, and what we will do, and attempting, as best we can, to anticipate what it will be like when we arrive.

If this is true of our earthly journeys, to destinations that often fall far short of our expectations, how much more should it be true of our journey to eternity, to the new heaven and the new earth, to a destination of unimaginable and unending glory. Certainly Peter thought it should, that believers should be 'looking for and hasting unto the coming of the day of God' (2 Pet. 3:12). It is worth asking ourselves how well we conform to the expectations of the apostle – and of the Holy Spirit.

In contrast with the wealth of detail that Scripture provides about the character and conditions of the Millennium, just a handful of passages give us details about the eternal state or, to use Peter's terminology, the day of God. There are two very brief references to the creation of the new heavens and new earth in the Old Testament (Isa. 65:17; 66:22). In the New Testament, three passages deal with the day of God – 1 Corinthians 15:24–28, 2 Peter 3:12–13, and Revelation 21 (some expositors include Revelation 21:9–22:5, while others, perhaps more persuasively, interpret these verses as speaking of the Millennium). Though these references are relatively sparse, they do provide us with a picture of the eternal state morally (2 Pet. 3), administratively (1 Cor. 15), and religiously (Rev. 21).

With the exception of 1 Corinthians 15, each of these passages speaks of a new creation. Expositors have long debated whether the existing creation will be utterly annihilated, and replaced with a creation that is totally new, or whether the language of Scripture envisages a re-creation of the existing cosmos. Both viewpoints have their supporters, but looking at Scripture as a whole, and taking care to distinguish between passages that speak of the Millennium and those that present the eternal state, it seems clear that the existing creation will be dissolved (Pss 97:5; 102:25–26; Isa. 13:13; 34:4; 51:6) and that the new creation will be a replacement for, not a renovation of, the cosmos that exists today. Whichever view we take, we must not miss the fact that we will spend eternity in a new creation, in a setting that is dramatically different to, and infinitely more blessed than, anything that has been known by the inhabitants of time.

In 2 Peter 3 the righteousness that will mark the new creation is stressed. Even the least cynical would have to acknowledge the endemic unrighteousness of the present creation. There is no human institution that is immune from the corrupting effects of man's unrighteousness. During the Millennium, Divine righteousness will reign, but it will be a righteousness imposed on mankind, and enforced with the most stringent of penalties. By contrast, righteousness will dwell in the new creation, residing there in a way that has never been true of the first creation. No tempter's voice will ever be heard, no sinful motive ever manifest, no unjust act ever committed. The perfect righteousness of God will be at home, resting upon all that goes on throughout the unending eternal day.

1 Corinthians 15:24–28 emphasise the Divine rule that will mark the day of God:

> Then cometh the end, when He shall have delivered up the kingdom to God, even the Father; when He shall have put down all rule and all authority and power. For He must reign, till He hath put all enemies under His feet. The last enemy that shall be destroyed is death. For He hath put all things under His feet. But when He saith all things are put under Him, it is manifest that He is excepted, which did put all things under Him. And when all things shall be subdued unto Him, then shall the Son also Himself be subject unto Him that put all things under Him, that God may be all in all.

The greatest purpose of the Millennium will be the vindication of Christ. His reign will display His authority, and demonstrate the truth of all that men challenged and denied. As the last Adam He will triumph where the first Adam failed. He will faithfully and successfully carry out the purpose of God right to the end. The end here is not the end of the age or dispensation. It is the end of time, the end of the old creation. At that point, when all things are in subjection, the last enemy destroyed, sin finally dealt with, and the old creation dissolved, Christ will willingly deliver the kingdom up to the Father. The mediatorial kingdom will be subsumed into the eternal and universal kingdom of God and, in the new creation, the triune God will be all in all.

Revelation 21:1-8 is perhaps the most detailed passage dealing with the eternal state. The apostle lists many things that will be absent: there will be no death, sorrow, crying, or pain (v. 4). Man will no longer be at a distance from God. The Temple with its mediating priesthood and sacrifices will no longer be needed. The 'tabernacle of God [will be] with men, and He will dwell with them, and they shall be His people, and God Himself shall be with them, and be their God' (Rev. 21:3). God will reside in the midst of His creation. His glory will be universally manifest – not now filling the Temple, but all of the new heaven and the new earth.

The greatness of our eternal dwelling is something that we, bound by the limits of time and the constraints of the flesh, cannot comprehend. But the contemplation of it ought to have a greater part in our lives than it does, and those Scriptures that outline its blessedness ought to be our continual contemplation and joy. And as we understand that this world and its glory are only transitory, that every material possession is only so much fuel for the purging fire 'what manner of persons ought [we] to be in all holy conversation and godliness' (2 Pet. 3:11)? And, even as we grasp that the temporal things that ensnare our hearts and enmesh our lives will shortly and certainly pass away, may we in truth look for and hasten to the day of God, looking, according to His promise for 'new heavens and a new earth, wherein dwelleth righteousness', heeding the exhortation of Scripture:

'Wherefore, beloved, seeing that ye look for such things, be diligent that ye may be found of Him in peace, without spot, and blameless' (vv. 13–14).

CHAPTER TWENTY-ONE

THE HOPE THAT IS IN YOU

THE HOPE AND HOPES OF THE BELIEVER

IN THE EARLY DECADES of the fourteenth century, the Italian poet Dante Alighieri wrote and published his *Inferno*. One of the three parts that make up his *Divine Comedy*, the poem records Dante's journey through hell. It is entirely a work of fantasy, with scant relationship to Biblical teaching. However, amongst all the grotesque punishments described by the poet, there is one detail that strikes a chilling note of reality. On the gates to hell Dante finds inscribed the phrase 'Abandon all hope, ye who enter here.' Despite the poet's ingenuity in devising appropriate punishments for the classes of sinners he imagines, it is the idea of a place without hope that is most haunting, the thing above all others that gives hell its horror.

In our gospel preaching we rightly emphasise the hopelessness of a lost eternity but we do well to remember that we speak to those who, even in time, are described as 'having no hope' (Eph. 2:12) and as 'others which have no hope' (1 Thess. 4:13). This world is filled with people without real hope. They desperately, despairingly seek hope, from their leaders, from their own escapist fantasies, from anywhere at all, but this vain pursuit provides nothing more than a temporary and illusory bulwark against the utter hopelessness of a sinful soul in a perishing world.

Amidst the counterfeit political and religious hopes of this world, the gospel stands solitary and unique as a message that imparts true hope. As believers whose faith is fixed on the Lord Jesus Christ, we have been given hope. We are 'begotten ... unto a lively hope' (1 Pet. 1:3), we 'have hope in Christ' (1 Cor. 15:19) and we 'rejoice in hope of the glory of God' (Rom. 5:2). With faith and love, hope is one of the Christian graces, the essential characteristics of a believer in the Lord Jesus. This hope ought to mark us out in a hopeless world.

At times, though, hope seems to be the forgotten grace, little thought of, and seldom mentioned. This may reflect the fact that hope, in the Biblical sense, is a subject that requires a comprehensive view of Scripture if we are to understand it correctly. We can turn to 1 Corinthians 13 for a definition of love, or to Hebrews 11 for definition and an extensive array of examples of faith. We do not have a single chapter dealing with hope in this way and so, to understand this vital concept, we must be prepared to work a little harder. It is worth remembering that hope is linked with the head and, by extension, with the mind in 1 Thessalonians 5:8, with the understanding in Ephesians 1:18, and with the reason in 1 Peter 3:15. It is truth for the head, as well as for the heart.

One of the most important steps in understanding the nature of hope is to draw a distinction between the hope and the hopes of the believer. As Christians, we have a glorious variety of hopes – of promised events that we look forward to. The Rapture, for example, is *a* hope of the believer; the manifestation of Christ is another. These events are the objects of our hope, of that disposition of mind that looks forward to the fulfilment of God's promises, and that makes it possible for us to live presently in the expectation of them. The hope of the believer, then, is this set of mind.

It is important to understand that this hope is a work of grace, brought about by the work of the Spirit of God. We all know people who are naturally optimistic by disposition, just as we know incurable pessimists. But the hope of the believer is not the result of an habitual disposition. Rather, as Romans 5 demonstrates, it is by faith 'we have access ... into this grace wherein we stand, and rejoice in hope of the glory of God' (v. 2) And the hope produced by the Spirit upon believing is nurtured and increased by the same Spirit:

> we glory in tribulations also: knowing that tribulation worketh patience; And patience, experience; and experience, hope: And hope maketh not ashamed; because the love of God is shed abroad in our hearts by the Holy Ghost which is given unto us' (vv. 3–5).

Later in the epistle, Paul stresses, once more, the supernatural origins and nature of hope: 'Now the God of hope fill you with all joy and peace in believing, that ye may abound in hope, through the power of the Holy Ghost' (Rom. 15:13).

The same chapter reveals a further vital feature of hope – it is founded upon the Word of God. We all have aspirations, there are events that each of us would love to see happen. But, unless these events are promised in Scripture, we cannot be said to hope for them in the Biblical sense. So it is that Paul reminds us that 'whatsoever things were written aforetime were written for our learning, that we through patience and comfort of the scriptures might have hope' (Rom. 15:4). Our hope must rest on a scriptural foundation if it is to have value, if, indeed, it is to be hope at all.

It follows from this that the hope of the believer is based on certainty. This is an important point because, in normal usage, hope indicates uncertainty. An unbeliever may hope to win the lottery: if he somehow knew he was going to win he would no longer hope, because, for him, hope implies uncertainty. The contrast with the hope of the believer could not be greater. We hope because we are certain, because the promises of God make us sure. This is the aspect of hope that the writer to the Hebrews gives expression to in chapter 6:

> Wherein God, willing more abundantly to shew unto the heirs of promise the immutability of His counsel, confirmed it by an oath: That by two immutable things, in which it was impossible for God to lie, we might have a strong consolation, who have fled for refuge to lay hold upon the hope set before us: Which hope we have as an anchor of the soul, both sure and stedfast, and which entereth into that within the vail; Whither the forerunner is for us entered, even Jesus (vv. 17–20).

These verses remind us of another feature of our hope – it makes the future relevant to the present. Our hope enters into what is heavenly and future, making it relevant to our present life, allowing us to live the here and now in the light of the then and there. Those things for which we hope are future: they have not happened yet, for if they had we would no longer hope for them – 'what a man seeth, why doth he yet hope for?' (Rom. 8:24). But hope links us to those things that are future, glorious, and eternal, making them effectual in our present life, giving us stability and security amidst the tempests and turmoil of time. And, just as the moment will come when faith will give way to sight, so too will hope give way to the full enjoyment of the reality of all that God has promised us. 'Now abideth faith, hope, charity', 1 Corinthians 13:13 reminds us, but the time will come when:

> *Constant FAITH, and holy HOPE shall dye,*
> *One lost in Certainty, and One in Joy.*
> (Matthew Prior)

Until that day may God grant us help to rejoice in hope (Rom. 12:12), not 'moved away from the hope of the gospel' (Col. 1:23), but manifesting that hope through that gospel in a dark and hopeless world.

Chapter Twenty-Two

'Able to Give an Answer'

THE THEME OF HOPE is a major preoccupation in Peter's first epistle. The epistle is addressed to scattered strangers and, however we choose to interpret this designation, it is likely that at least some of those to whom Peter wrote would have been, in effect, refugees. Certainly, they were 'in heaviness through manifold temptations' (1:6). Dispersed from their homes and loved ones and called to live for God in a hostile society these believers needed to be reminded of the hope that they had, a hope of things far above and beyond the distresses of their present existence. It is, perhaps, for this reason that Peter begins his epistle by reminding the believers of the basis of that hope. In chapter one he outlines for them the ABC of their hope.

Assured by the Resurrection

Throughout the first chapter of the epistle, Peter emphasises the foundational importance of the resurrection of Christ to the hope of the believer. So, in verse 3, he blesses God Who has 'begotten us again unto a lively hope by the resurrection of Jesus Christ from the dead.' Later, he draws a similar connection, reminding his readers that they have believed in the God Who raised Christ 'up from the dead, and gave Him glory; that your faith and hope might be in God' (v. 21). For Peter the resurrection of Christ from the dead underwrites every promise of God. If the stone, the tomb, the Roman seal, and death itself could not stand in God's way, what obstacle could? Christ's resurrection assures the believer that, no matter what the obstacles presented by circumstances, no matter how hopeless their existence seemed, the power of God – that same power that raised Christ from the dead – is able to triumph, and see the promises of God fulfilled. This makes the hope of the believer starkly different from the hopes of the world. The unsaved hope for the best – they hope because of uncertainty. The Saviour's empty tomb means that the believer hopes because of certainty, the certainty that what God has promised He will perform. The resurrection assures our hope.

BASED ON SCRIPTURE

If the resurrection assures our hope, then the Scriptures direct it. Peter makes it clear that Christian hope is based firmly on the foundation of Scripture. It is for this reason that he reminds his readers of the writers of Old Testament prophecy who only dimly understood 'what, or what manner of time the Spirit of Christ which was in them did signify, when it testified beforehand the sufferings of Christ, and the glory that should follow' (v. 11). The special blessing for saints of the present dispensation is that these Scriptures, so obscure even to those that wrote them, provide the basis for our hope. The hope of a believer is not an optimistic feeling that things will turn out as we would like them to. Rather, it is a confidence based on the Divinely revealed Word of God, that word that 'liveth and abideth for ever' (v. 23) and that 'endureth for ever' (v. 25). Hope that is without the Word of God does not deserve the name. We only stand firm for the future with Scripture as our foundation.

CENTRED ON CHRIST

The believer's hope is centred on Christ. This is true, not only in the sense that His death brings us salvation, and thus hope, or that His resurrection assures our hope, but also because He is the sum of our hope. We are accustomed to think of the hopes of the Church, to begin at the Rapture and work through the riches of prophetic revelation. But all these precious hopes are summed up in Christ. We do expect the Rapture, just as we long for the manifestation of Christ, but it should be true of us that we look not for an event but for a Person, not for 'it' but for 'Him.' This certainly is the emphasis of Peter's teaching in this chapter, as he directs the eye of the believer to the 'appearing of Jesus Christ: Whom having not seen, ye love; in whom, though now ye see Him not, yet believing, ye rejoice with joy unspeakable and full of glory' (vv. 7–8). A few verses later, he once more centres their expectation on Christ, exhorting them to 'hope to the end for the grace that is to be brought unto you at the revelation of Jesus Christ' (v. 13). These verses do have a specific event in view – it is the return of Christ to the earth that Peter anticipates here. But the focus is on Christ as the centre and the sum of the believer's hope.

THE HOPE THAT IS IN YOU

This, then, is the sort of hope that Peter has in mind when, in the third chapter of the epistle, he charges his readers to 'be ready always to give an answer to every man that asketh you a reason of the hope that is in you with meekness and fear' (3:15). This verse adds some detail to our understanding of the believer's hope.

Firstly, it is an essential hope. Peter takes it for granted that this hope is part of the experience of each individual believer. And this should be so. One of the greatest things that salvation does for sinners is to bring hope. One of the saddest descriptions of the unsaved is given to us in 1 Thessalonians 4:13, where Paul speaks of them as 'others which have no hope.' By contrast, all believers have been 'begotten ... unto a lively hope' (1 Pet. 1:3). It is an essential and indispensible part of the believer's life.

But the hope that Peter speaks of is also an evident hope. He envisages that those who observed the lives of these believers would be struck by the hope that was evident in the character of these beleaguered believers, in spite of contrary circumstances. And we, in our own age should similarly live lives of evident hope. It is unthinkable that this should not be so – that believers (who alone have hope in a hopeless world) should not live so that that hope is evident to all is a tragedy indeed. Peter expects that it will not be so in the life of these believers.

And when they are asked, they should be ready to prove that the believer's hope is an explicable hope, to confidently 'give an answer' of the hope that they so clearly display. Based on the foundation laid by Peter in the first chapter, the believer's hope is not 'pie in the sky' refusal to face reality. Rather, it is a reasonable response to the power and the promises of God. And we should be ready to defend it as such, ready, at a moment's notice, to account for that which makes us distinct in a hopeless world.

The hope of the believer assures us: it ought not to make us arrogant. It is Peter's desire that the saints be confident but never cocky in the declaration of their hope – their answer was to be given 'with meekness and fear'. The man who had once sought to defend the truth, to defend Christ himself, with a drawn sword has learned that there is a right way and a correct spirit in which to testify to the truth of God.

Peter's desire for the scattered and suffering believers to whom his letter was first written is God's for each of us today. By His grace He has brought to us a hope unique to His own. It is His desire that we should understand it with our minds, enjoy it in our hearts, live it in our lives, and explain it with our lips, to His glory, and to the blessing of others.

Chapter Twenty-Three

Conclusion

PETER'S SECOND EPISTLE is filled with foreboding. As the apostle anticipates his death he warns of those who will come – 'false teachers ... who privily shall bring in damnable heresies' (2:1) and 'scoffers, walking after their own lusts' (3:3). He anticipates days filled with the darkness of departure. His words paint a gloomy picture, but not a hopeless one. Amidst the surrounding shade shines a brilliant light:

> We have also a more sure word of prophecy; whereunto ye do well that ye take heed, as unto a light that shineth in a dark place, until the day dawn, and the day star arise in your hearts (2 Pet. 1:19).

The light of Scripture, the 'exceeding great and precious promises' of God (1:4), is both a comfort and guide, dispelling the darkness, and directing the believer's course until the glorious moment of daybreak.

Peter's words describe a Divine provision: 'prophecy came not in old time by the will of man: but holy men of God spake as they were moved by the Holy Ghost' (1:21). But even as he describes Divine provision, he highlights human responsibility. We are to 'take heed' to this 'more sure word of prophecy'. Prophecy that remains shut away in the clean pages of our Bible will not profit us. It is as we take heed to God's Word, carefully and painstakingly reading, re-reading, and studying it, that we will know the comfort and the clarity of the light that it alone provides. And all of prophetic Scripture demands and rewards this careful study. In chapter 3 of the epistle, Peter brings before us the entire prophetic programme, from the arrival of the day of the Lord (v. 10), to the commencement of the eternal day of God (v. 12). He directs his readers not to a few gleams of prophetic truth, but to the full-orbed radiance of God's great prophetic plan.

In Peter's final words we have a mandate for the careful and comprehensive study of prophetic Scripture – not because it will make us more clever or better informed, but because it should make us more hopeful and more holy. It is our prayer that the overview provided in this volume may have whetted our appetite for the study of this vital vein of Divine truth, and that this truth will thrill our souls and shape our lives as it ought. With this in mind, the remainder of this chapter will outline some useful books to assist our study of prophecy.

The range of books on prophecy available to the student of Scripture is vast and varied. Care is always advisable when selecting books, and the range of prophetic interpretation in circulation means that it is well to be especially cautious when buying books on prophecy. In particular, sensationalising works that attempt to interpret prophecy in light of current events – or *vice versa* – are best avoided. It is generally true that by their covers ye shall know them, and while sober typography and sober theology do not always go together, the presence of exclamation marks on the front cover is almost invariably a reliable indicator of an unhelpful book.

Over the past decade or so, a wave of 'rapture novels' has appeared. These books purport to present the events that will take place before the Rapture and during the Tribulation. These should be avoided. Though they may seem like a low-effort introduction to prophecy, these novels contain much questionable teaching, and will be of little help to the believer who wants to gain a Biblical understanding of prophecy.

It should go without saying that the best book to impart a Biblical understanding of prophecy is the Bible. We often allow ourselves to be daunted by the complexity of prophetic truth, by its presentation in types and symbols, and by the way it permeates all of Scripture. There is a great deal of truth to grasp and systematize, and there is no doubt that other books can help us to do this. They should, however, be used as an adjunct to reading the Bible for ourselves, and not as a substitute for it. And while there will be much that at first seems obscure, the study of and meditation upon Scripture will yield enlightenment 'line upon line; here a little, and there a little' (Isa. 28:13). Such study is essential if we are to be properly grounded in our understanding of prophecy.

The key to studying a subject like prophecy is to get the big picture – the overarching structure – clear in our minds, and then to fill in the detail of the picture. A grasp of dispensational truth is vital to a proper understanding of Scripture. In particular, a clear grasp of prophetic teaching is heavily dependent on distinguishing things that differ. An introduction to the biblical truth of the dispensations is provided by the author's *The Dispensations: God's Plan for the Ages*.

The books of Daniel and Revelation are central to our understanding of Bible prophecy, and commentaries on these volumes are especially useful. Jim Allen's commentary on Revelation in the 'What the Bible Teaches' series, and his *Daniel Reconsidered* are careful and detailed expositions of these two challenging books. John F. Walvoord's treatments of these books are also worth having and H.A. Ironside is as readable on these books as he always is, and is simple without being simplistic.

The prophecy of seventy weeks, revealed by the angel Gabriel to Daniel is, as we have seen, the backbone of prophetic revelation. A clear understanding of the prophetic structure revealed to Daniel allows us to get the rest of prophecy properly in its place. A number of works deal in detail with this prophecy. Sir Robert Anderson's *The Coming Prince* is the classic work in this regard. Harold Hoehner refined Anderson's calculations in his *Chronological Aspects of the Life of Christ*. Alva McClain's *Daniel's Prophecy of the Seventy Weeks* is a concise but helpful treatment of the issue.

There is one book on prophecy that unquestionably falls into the select category of 'must-have' books for Bible study. J.D. Pentecost is always worth reading, but *Things to Come* is perhaps his most valuable work. It provides a structured and comprehensive overview of Biblical prophecy, and builds its conclusions on the careful exegesis of Scripture. Pentecost also quotes widely from other authors, and his footnotes often serve as valuable pointers to additional reading.

F.A. Tatford's *God's Programme for the Ages* is a useful brief introduction to prophetic and – to a lesser extent – dispensational truth. His commentaries on the Minor Prophets provide brief but lucid introductions to these oftentimes neglected books. His commentaries on

Zechariah – *Prophet of the Myrtle Grove* – and Ezekiel – *Dead Bones Live* – are longer than the other volumes in the series, and provide detailed exposition of these two important books.

The millennial reign of Christ is a subject that runs right through Scripture. A positive and comprehensive account of Kingdom teaching, including – but not limited to – the Kingdom in its millennial manifestation, is provided by Alva McClain's classic *The Glory of the Kingdom*. A detailed critique of amillennial teaching is provided by David McAllister's series of articles, 'Amillennialism Examined', which appeared in *Assembly Testimony* from July 1995 to March 1997. Another helpful series on the subject – 'A Millennial or A-Millennial Future: Which?' – appeared in *Truth & Tidings* from February to December 2010. Both series are available online, and provide a concise and cogent critique of an erroneous doctrine that has plagued believers since the days of Augustine.

This list is far from being exhaustive, but it does highlight some works that will help us to understand the framework of prophetic revelation. Filling in that framework will keep us busy – and hopeful, and holy, and happy – until we arrive, at last, in the day of eternity.

Appendix

The Days of Scripture

THE WORD OF GOD divides time in a number of different ways. Among these, the Bible speaks of a number of days that mark the future of our universe. These are 'man's day' (1 Cor. 4:3, JND), the 'day of Christ' (Phil. 1:10), the 'day of the Lord' (1 Thess. 5:2) and 'the day of God' (2 Pet. 3:12). Grasping the distinction between these different days will greatly assist our ability to understand God's prophetic programme.

It may be worthwhile to begin by stating what will seem obvious to most: these expressions do not refer to a twenty-four hour day. In Hebrew and Greek, the word 'day' has a range of meanings, from part of a day, a twenty-four hour period, to a longer period of time that is marked by a particular unifying character (e.g. 'the day of salvation' 2 Cor. 6:2; 'the day of eternity' 2 Pet. 3:18, JND).

MAN'S DAY

'Man's day' is, perhaps, the least familiar, but an examination of the phrase in context is helpful to understanding the other expressions. In 1 Corinthians 4:3, rendered literally, Paul states 'it is the very smallest matter that I be examined of you or of man's day'. Other translations interpret the phrase 'of man's day' as 'man's judgement' or 'any human court'. The literal translation preserves the contrast that Paul is drawing between man's day, in this chapter, and 'the day' in 3:13. Paul is not just contrasting the present with the future; he is also contrasting man's day – the present period in which things are judged by man's standards – with a future day when Christ will determine the criteria for judgement. So, the terms day of the Lord, day of Christ, and day of God direct our attention to the judgement and administration that applies in each of these periods.

THE DAY OF THE LORD

The Old Testament prophets speak frequently of the day of the LORD (e.g. Isa. 2:12; 13:6; 13:9; Jer. 46:10; Ezek. 13:5; 30:3; Joel 1:15; 2:1, 11, 31; 3:14; Amos 5:18, 20; Obad. 15; Zeph. 1:7, 14; Zech. 14:1; Mal. 4:5), and their descriptions are well summarised by Zephaniah:

> The great day of the LORD is near, it is near, and hasteth greatly ... That day is a day of wrath, a day of trouble and distress, a day of wasteness and desolation, a day of darkness and gloominess, a day of clouds and thick darkness, A day of the trumpet and alarm against the fenced cities, and against the high towers (1:14–16).

This period, so vividly evoked in prophecy, will be marked by Jehovah's judgement upon Israel and the nations, and by the direct Divine administration of earth.

The commencement of the day of the Lord is described in 1 Thessalonians 5:2–3: 'the day of the Lord so cometh as a thief in the night. For when they shall say, Peace and safety; then sudden destruction cometh upon them, as travail upon a woman with child; and they shall not escape.' It will commence silently and stealthily, breaking upon mankind in a time of apparent security. The apostle's use of labour pains as a simile for the throes that will enfold the globe is significant. It is the same word used by the Lord Jesus when He spoke of 'the beginning of sorrows' that would mark the first three and a half years of the Tribulation (Mt. 24:8). So the day of the Lord will commence at the same time as the Tribulation: perhaps when the Lion of the tribe of Judah takes the sealed scroll (Rev. 5:7).

Peter provides us with the detail of the duration and conclusion of the day of the Lord. Using very similar language to Paul he reminds his readers that 'the day of the Lord will come as a thief in the night; in the which the heavens shall pass away with a great noise, and the elements shall melt with fervent heat, the earth also and the works that are therein shall be burned up' (2 Pet. 3:10). So, the day of the Lord extends from the beginning of the Tribulation, through the Millennium, and on to the moment when God will fold up the heavens and the earth like a worn-out garment (Heb. 1:11–12).

There are a number of occasions in Scripture where the phrase 'day of the Lord' is used in a slightly different way. In Zechariah 14:1 the prophet warns the city of Jerusalem: 'Behold, the day of the LORD cometh, and thy spoil shall be divided in the midst of thee.' The phrase translated 'the day of the LORD' or the 'the day of Jehovah' in most English translations is not the same as that used elsewhere in the Old Testament. Literally translated it is 'a day cometh – the LORD's', and it is perhaps best translated 'a day is coming for the LORD'.* The remainder of the chapter makes it clear that this day for the Lord is the day of His appearing, when He will 'go forth, and fight against those nations, as when he fought in the day of battle' (v. 3), returning to the scene of His ascension to succour the faithful saints of the beleaguered remnant, and to abash the assembled military might of the nations of the earth. That day will

---

* As it is in the ESV, NASB, ISV, and JND.

truly be a day for Him, as He returns in victory to the scene of His rejection. His return will bring swift and irresistible judgement upon the nations, but the focus of this great chapter is upon the blessing that He will bring; the relief and restoration to a weary and wounded earth, so that 'there shall be no more utter destruction' (v. 11) but 'the LORD shall be king over all the earth: in that day shall there be one LORD, and His name one' (v. 9).

Another distinctive usage of the 'day of the LORD' is found in Joel 2:31, and quoted by Peter on the day of Pentecost:

> The sun shall be turned into darkness, and the moon into blood, before that great and notable day of the Lord come (Acts 2:20).

Here, the expression 'great and notable' qualifies 'the day of the Lord'. It is clear that this great and notable day is distinct from the 'day of the Lord', in the more general sense that normally applies. This day – so great, so conspicuous, or even glorious – takes place after the sun 'turned into darkness, and the moon into blood'. Matthew 24:29–30 allow us to place this event in the wider chronology of prophetic time:

> Immediately after the tribulation of those days shall the sun be darkened, and the moon shall not give her light, and the stars shall fall from heaven, and the powers of the heavens shall be shaken: And then shall appear the sign of the Son of man in heaven: and then shall all the tribes of the earth mourn, and they shall see the Son of man coming in the clouds of heaven with power and great glory.

Comparing these passages makes it clear that the 'great and notable day of the Lord', described in Joel 2:31, is the day of Christ's return, the day spoken of by Zechariah as a day coming for the Lord. As ever, careful attention to the text and the context of Scripture is vital, to allow us to distinguish the things that differ, and to prevent us from conflating or confounding the precise detail of the prophetic outline.

THE DAY OF GOD

It is Peter who tells us about the day of God. In 2 Peter 3, he looks beyond the day of the Lord into eternity:

> Looking for and hasting unto the coming of the day of God, wherein the heavens being on fire shall be dissolved, and the elements shall melt with fervent heat. Nevertheless we, according to his promise, look for new heavens and a new earth, wherein dwelleth righteousness (vv. 12–13).

This is one of the few glimpses we get into the eternal state, into 'the day of eternity' (2 Pet. 3:18, JND). In that day, Christ will have delivered the kingdom up to His Father, and God shall 'be all in all' (1 Cor. 15:28).

Thus, in the three days we have considered we have a chronological sequence through time, extending from the present (man's day), through the Tribulation and Millennium (the day of the Lord), and on to the eternal state (the day of God).

In addition to these days, the apostle Paul uses a number of terms to describe a coming day of review (1 Cor. 1:8; 3:13), reward (2 Tim. 4:6–8), rejoicing (Phil. 2:16), and rest (Phil. 1:6, 10). These are the 'day of Christ' (Phil. 1:10; 2:16) the 'day of Jesus Christ' (Phil. 1:6), the 'day of our Lord Jesus Christ' (1 Cor. 1:8), the 'day of the Lord Jesus' (1 Cor. 5:5), and 'that day' (2 Tim. 1:12; 4:8). It is significant that only Paul speaks of this day. Like the doctrine of the Church, the day of Christ is unknown in Old Testament Scripture – it applies only to those who are 'in Christ' (Rom. 8:10; 1 Cor. 15:18; 2 Cor. 5:17, etc.). Just as the Church is a heavenly body, the day of Christ is a heavenly day. Its character stands in stark contrast to the terror associated with the day of the Lord. It is looked and longed for. It motivated the labours of the great apostle, and it should, likewise, be always on our horizons as a spur to our spiritual exercise.

Scripture gives us little explicit detail as to the timing of this day. However, it is clear, from the features mentioned above, that it must take place after the Rapture, and before the Church appears with Christ in manifestation. It seems that the day of Christ will run throughout the period of the Tribulation, but with a heavenly, rather than an earthly focus. In this day, the judgement seat of Christ and the marriage of the Lamb will take place.

This is a brief look at these important Scriptural concepts. The reader should search the Scriptures, comparing scripture with scripture, in order to grasp the vital details and distinctions of these Divinely-appointed days.

www.ingramcontent.com/pod-product-compliance
Lightning Source LLC
Chambersburg PA
CBHW050825160426
43192CB00010B/1894